NATO 'FAIR TRIAL' SAFEGUARDS

NATO 'FAIR TRIAL' SAFEGUARDS: PRECURSOR TO AN INTERNATIONAL BILL OF PROCEDURAL RIGHTS

by

ROBERT B. ELLERT

Lieutenant Colonel, J.A.G.C., U.S. Army
S.J.D. (The George Washington University)
Postgraduate Diploma in Law
(Kings College, University of London)
B.A., B.C.L, (College of William and Mary)

SPRINGER-SCIENCE+BUSINESS MEDIA, B.V.
1963

To Johanna

This work was done in partial fulfillment of the requirements for the degree of Doctor of Juridical Science awarded by the Graduate School of Public Law of the George Washington University, Washington, D.C.

ISBN 978-94-017-5726-3 *ISBN 978-94-017-6079-9 (eBook)*
DOI 10.1007/978-94-017-6079-9

Originally published by Martinus Nijhoff, The Hague, Netherlands in 1963
Softcover reprint of the hardcover 1st edition 1963

TABLE OF CONTENTS

CHAPTER I

INTRODUCTION

World War II and its aftermath demonstrated the futility of planning military defense in terms of an individual country. The Western World needed a new approach to preserve its security. In March 1946 Winston Churchill in a speech at Fulton, Missouri, made a proposal for a defensive alliance to protect the West in the cold war.[1]

In succeeding years the United States recognized the necessity for such a defensive alliance and that the survival of the United States and of the other free nations of the North Atlantic Community depended on collective security. Truly, as was stated by Secretary of State Dulles, independence today could only be achieved by interdependence.[2]

On 4 April 1949 the desire of the United States, Canada, Belgium, Denmark, France, Iceland, Italy, Luxembourg, the Netherlands, Norway Portugal, and the United Kingdom to share the problem of mutual defence was formalized by the North Atlantic Treaty.[3] In 1952 Greece and Turkey joined NATO,[4] and in 1955, so did the Federal Republic of Germany.[5] This Agreement was a partnership of politically free and economically stable nations joined together for the purpose of exercising those political, economic, and military sanctions necessary to defend against communist aggression and expansion.

This all important defensive alliance contemplated an unprecedented peacetime stationing of the forces of one party in the territory of another.[6] What, however, was to be the status of such visiting forces?

[1] *The New York Times*, March 6, 1946, p. 4.

[2] Statement of Secretary Dulles to Edgar McInnis, President of the Canadian Institute of International Affairs on June 23, 1958, and reiterated in an address entitled, *NATO: Interdependence in Action* before the Atlantic Treaty Association, Boston, Mass., on September 27, 1958 (See 39 *Dept State Bull.* 62, 571 (1958)).

[3] *T.I.A.S.* 1964 (Entered into force August 24, 1949).

[4] Protocol to the North Atlantic Treaty on the Accession of Greece and Turkey, *T.I.A.S.* 2390 (Entered into force February 15, 1952).

[5] Protocol to the North Atlantic Treaty on the Accession of the Federal Republic of Germany, *T.I.A.S.* 3428 (Entered into force 5 May 1955).

[6] Arts. 3 and 5, *T.I.A.S.* 1964, *supra.*

Decision makers could not justify to their peoples the need for according to visiting forces in peacetime the sweeping immunities from local law which were granted to them *in extremis* during World War II.[7] Yet, the forces of a sending state, even in peacetime, needed certain functional immunities from local law in order to carry out properly the mutual defense requirements of NATO. Consequently it was necessary to negotiate a balanced agreement based upon reciprocity which more or less precisely defined the rights, duties, and obligations of a visiting force while stationed in the host state.

On June 19, 1951, the *Agreement Between the Parties to the North Atlantic Treaty Regarding the Status of Their Forces* (*SOF*) was signed in London and eventually ratified by 13 nations.[8] This Agreement sets out the rights, duties, and obligations of the signatories in several areas of importance, including such matters as passport and visa regulations;[9] identity cards, movement orders, and expulsion of undesirables;[10] drivers licenses;[11] payment of claims;[12] procurement of goods, services, facilities and labor;[13] criminal jurisdiction;[14] duty free imports;[15] and foreign exchange regulations.[16]

The criminal jurisdictional provision is the heart of the agreement. It is an integral segment of the give and take scheme of mutual defense which is the keystone of NATO. This provision sets out a formula which resolves the sensitive issue of the exercise of criminal jurisdiction over members of a force who commit offenses in the host country over which there is concurrent jurisdiction by the sending and receiving states.[17] Under this formula the primary right to exercise jurisdiction

[7] See Hearings Before the Committee on Foreign Affairs, House of Representatives, 84th Cong., 1st and 2d Sess. on H. J. Res. 309, Status of Forces Agreements (1955–1956) 143 for a summary of wartime status of forces agreements.

[8] *T.I.A.S.* 2846 (Entered into force August 24, 1953). Dates of ratification are as follows: United States-July 24, 1953; France, Norway, and Belgium-Aug. 23, 1953; Canada-Sept. 27, 1953; The Netherlands-Dec. 18, 1953; Luxembourg-April 18, 1954; United Kingdom-June 12, 1954; Turkey-June 17, 1954; Denmark-June 27, 1954; Greece-Aug. 25, 1954; Portugal-Dec. 22, 1955; Italy-Jan. 21, 1956 (Federal Republic of Germany-ratification not finally completed.)

[9] Par. 1, Art. III.

[10] Pars. 2 and 5, Art. III.

[11] Art. IV.

[12] Art. VIII.

[13] Art. IX.

[14] Art. VII.

[15] Art. XI.

[16] Art. XIV.

[17] Par. 3, Art. VII. The text of this paragraph is as follows:

3. In cases where the right to exercise jurisdiction is concurrent the following rules shall apply:

(a) The military authorities of the sending State shall have the primary right in such cases is apportioned on a reciprocal basis to accommodate the paramount interests of the sending and receiving states. The sending state may try offenses committed by its forces against its property or nationals or arising out of an act or omission done in the performance of official duty. On the other hand, the host country has the primary right to try a member of a visiting force for offenses committed against its nationals, such as murder, rape, or robbery, which are calculated to arouse the ire and resentment of a local population.[18]

to exercise jurisdiction over a member of a force or of a civilian component in relation to

(i) offences solely against the property or security of that State, or offences solely against the person or property of another member of the force or civilian component of that State or of a dependent;

(ii) offences arising out of any act or omission done in the performance of official duty.

(b) In the case of any other offence the authorities of the receiving State shall have the primary right to exercise jurisdiction.

(c) If the State having the primary right decides not to exercise jurisdiction, it shall notify the authorities of the other State as soon as practicable. The authorities of the State having the primary right shall give sympathetic consideration to a request from the authorities of the other State for a waiver of its right in cases where that other State considers such waiver to be of particular importance.

[18] In the United States this criminal jurisdiction formula, which subjected United States servicemen to trial, sentencing and confinement by the authorities of the other signatories to the Agreement, was severely criticized on the ground that it was contrary to the rule of customary international law that friendly foreign troops are immune from the jurisdiction of a host nation in which they are stationed with its consent. This criticism was generated largely because the United States under NATO is primarily a sending state; that is, the number of United States forces stationed in other NATO countries is disproportionately greater than the approximately 12,000 foreign troops stationed in the United States during the course of a year. (See Hearings Before the Committee on Foreign Affairs, House of Representatives, 84th Cong., 1st and 2d Sess. on H. J. Res. 309, Status of Forces Agreements (1955–1956) 271 for a breakdown of the various categories of foreign troops in the United States.) If there had been an equal number of foreign troops stationed in the United States committing offenses such as rape, murder, and robbery against United States nationals, it is probable that there would have been no serious criticism of the formula as in such cases the United States would have had the primary right to try such foreign personnel.

See debate set out in 99 *Cong. Rec.* 8724–8782, (1953). At that time an amendment reserving exclusive jurisdiction over United States forces abroad to United States courts-martial was rejected by a vote of fifty-three to twenty-seven. 99 *Cong. Rec.* 8782 (1953).

For a presentation of the argument that under international law friendly foreign troops are immune from the jurisdiction of another nation where they are stationed with its consent see King, "Jurisdiction Over Friendly Armed Forces," 36 *Am. J. Int'l L.* 539 (1942) and King, "Further Developments Concerning Jurisdiction Over Friendly Foreign Armed Forces," 40 *Am. J. Int'l L.* 257 (1944).

For a rebuttal of this argument see Supplementary Hearings Before the Committee on Foreign Relations, U.S. Senate, 83rd Cong., 1st Sess., On Status of Forces of the North Atlantic Treaty (June 24, 1953) 2–59; and Hearings Before the Committee on Foreign Affairs, House of Representatives, 84th Cong., 1st and 2d Sess. on H. J. Res. 309, Status of Forces Agreements (1955–1956) Pt. 1, 139; Barton, "Foreign Armed Forces; Immunity from Criminal Jurisdiction," 27 *Brit. Y. B. Int'l L.* 186 (1950); Schwartz, "International Law and the Status of Forces Agreements," 53 *Colum. L. Rev.* 1091 (1953).

It should be noted that regardless of this controversy, the criminal jurisdiction formula

The intent of the decision makers to balance the interests of the sending and receiving states is further manifested by the provision in the NATO SOF Agreement which provides that a member of a visiting force prosecuted by a receiving state is entitled to certain "fair trial" safeguards.[19] This provision insures that a member of a visiting force will have the right to certain minimum procedural safeguards even though tried by a receiving state whose system of law might be different from that of the sending state. These safeguards are as follows:

(a) to a prompt and speedy trial;
(b) to be informed, in advance of trial, of the specific charge or charges made against him;
(c) to be confronted with the witnesses against him;
(d) to have compulsory process for obtaining witnesses in his favor, if they are within the jurisdiction of the receiving State;
(e) to have legal representation of his own choice for his defense or to have free or assisted legal representation under the conditions prevailing for the time being in the receiving State;
(f) if he considers it necessary, to have the services of a competent interpreter; and
(g) to communicate with a representative of the Government of the sending State and, when the rules of the court permit, to have such a representative present at his trial.

Based on the precedent of the NATO SOF Agreement these procedural safeguards were also incorporated into bilateral status of forces agreements between the United States and Japan,[20] Pakistan,[21] Nicaragua,[22] Libya,[23] Iceland,[24] the West Indies,[25] and Australia (Nauru Island).[26]

set out in the NATO SOF Agreement is an expression of positive international law. Whether it represents poor bargaining or practical statesmanship on the part of the United States, it must be accepted.

19 Par. 9, Art. VII.

20 Agreement under Article VI of the Treaty of Mutual Cooperation and Security, January 19, 1960, *T.I.A.S.* 4510.

21 Establishment of Communications Unit in Pakistan, July 18, 1959, *T.I.A.S.* 4281.

22 Establishment of Loran Transmitting Station in Nicaragua, Sept. 5, 1958, *T.I.A.S.* 4106.

23 Agreement Between the United States of America and the Government of the United Kingdom of Libya, Sept. 9, 1954, *T.I.A.S.* 3107.

24 Annex on the Status of United States Personnel and Property to the Defense Agreement Between the United States of America and the Republic of Iceland, May 8, 1951, *T.I.A.S.* 2295.

25 Agreement Between the United States of America and the Federation of The West Indies, United States Defense Areas in the Federation of the West Indies, February 10, 1961, *T.I.A.S.* 4734.

26 Weather Station, Nauru Island Agreement Between the United States of America

The inclusion of these "fair trial" safeguards in the NATO and other SOF agreements and their day to day application in different legal systems in literally thousands of cases each year represents a unique breakthrough in the implementation of human rights. It has been because of a lack of such implementation that the purpose of the United Nations with regard to the promotion and observance of human rights has been largely unfulfilled.[27]

Notwithstanding the unanimity of members of the General Assembly of the United Nations on December 10, 1948 in proclaiming the *Universal Declaration of Human Rights* as a "common standard of achievement for all peoples and all nations,"[28] there was a general repudiation of the idea that it imposed a legal obligation on nations to respect the human rights and fundamental freedoms which it proclaimed.[29] In this respect the United States representative stated, "In giving our approval to the declaration today, it is of primary importance that we keep clearly in mind the basic character of the document. It is not a treaty, it is not an international agreement. It is not and does not purport to be a statement of law or of legal obligation. It is a declaration of basic principles of human rights and freedoms, to be stamped with the approval of the General Assembly by a formal vote of its members, and to serve as a common standard of achievement for all peoples of all nations."[30]

The conversion of the *Declaration of Human Rights* into a body of binding obligations in the form of an international Bill of Rights has proved to be a difficult task.[31] It was undertaken under the auspices of the United Nations in 1947 and is still far from completion. Besides numerous political points which have created areas of disagreement among nations, such as the right of petition by individuals,[32] the prep-

and Australia on behalf of the Administering Authority (comprising the United Kingdom, Australia, and New Zealand) of Nauru Island, Feb. 25, 1958, *T.I.A.S.* 4001.

[27] See *Journal of the Economic and Social Council*, First Year, No. 29, p. 521 (1946).

[28] Preamble to *The Universal Declaration of Human Rights*.

[29] See H. Lauterpacht, *International Law and Human Rights*, 276, 394–428 (1950) for a detailed analysis of the rejection of the *Universal Declaration of Human Rights* as a legal instrument and where he expresses the view that the Declaration does not possess, and does not purport to possess, legal force or authority and that its moral significance is controversial.

[30] 19 *Dept State Bull.* 751 (1948).

[31] See H. Lauterpacht, *op. cit. supra* note 29, at 273–280 for a summary of the progress of the *International Bill of Rights* within the United Nations and its negative results.

[32] On this issue the Commission on Human Rights were equally divided. The states voting in favor of a resolution laying down that the right of petition by individuals, groups, and organizations should be recognized forthwith in a proposed "covenant" of Human Rights were: Australia, Denmark, France, Guatemala, India, Lebanon, the

aration and drafting of such a bill of rights has been complicated by the fact that the concepts underlying basic civil liberties and safeguards are so general in character that they are subject to diverse interpretations, not just in the different major legal systems but also in different states belonging to the same major legal system.[33] The experience of the United Nations in this endeavor compels the conclusion that an international Bill of Rights will not spring into existence full-panoplied. Rather an informal "backdoor" approach is indicated.[34] Individual rights must first gain acceptance in practice among nations which have different political and legal systems, traditions, and cultures. Such practice will refine the concept of such rights to the point where an acceptable universal basis may be formulated.

The main purpose of this inquiry is to suggest an informal approach whereby the extensive practice of the United States, the NATO nations, and other nations during the past eight years in the implementation of the "fair trial" safeguards contained in the various status of forces agreements in different systems of law may be utilized to achieve in one small area of individual rights where there is disagreement among nations an orderly modification of international law which would lead ultimately to universal acceptance of such rights in an international Bill of Procedural Rights.

The area chosen comprises the minimum procedural safeguards to be accorded an alien prosecuted by a host country. It will be demonstrated that there is a definite dichotomy between two groups of nations as to the criteria to be applied in determining the minimum procedural safeguards which a state must accord in the prosecution of an alien in order to avoid international responsibility for a denial thereof.

A method will be suggested whereby the practice of the United States and other nations in the implementation of the SOF "fair trial" safeguards in different systems of law may be utilized to obtain the agreement of both groups of nations to certain procedural safeguards to be accorded in the prosecution of an alien. It is believed that after such accord has been reached international practice with respect to these

Philippines, and Uruguay. Those voting against were: China, Egypt, Iran, the Ukraine, the USSR, the United Kingdom, the United States, and Yugoslavia, *id.* 279.

[33] See Jenks, *The Common Law of Mankind* 165 (1958) for a discussion of the great difficulties, including a self-determination clause, which have complicated the formulation of a covenant on human rights.

[34] This term was used by Major General Charles L. Decker, The Judge Advocate of the Army, in a Law Day speech at Colorado Springs, Colorado, on 1 May 1959 to describe the succesful implementation of the NATO "fair trial" safeguards by local United States military lawyers and local civilian authorities of foreign countries.

mutually agreed safeguards will establish among nations having different legal systems a common denominator as to the substance and meaning of each safeguard. Once this common denominator has been formalized the procedural safeguards in issue would be ripe for codification in an international Bill of Procedural Rights for all persons.

A subordinate purpose of this inquiry is to consider the remedies United States personnel [35] would have under international law and United States domestic law in the event they were denied one of the "fair trial" safeguards set out in paragraph 9 of Article VII of the NATO SOF Agreement.

The method of inquiry used will be largely empirical. It will emphasize the development of international law as a decision-making process in which the decision makers are influenced by many variables; as a flow of decisions in which community prescriptions are formulated, invoked, and in fact applied in the promotion of community policies. In assessing the validity of legal doctrines not only the structures and processes of formal authority but also those of effective power and of their interrelations will be considered.[36] Specifically, the practice of the United States and nations whose systems of law are different from that of the United States during the past eight years in the implementation of the "fair trial" safeguards set out in the NATO SOF Agreement in several thousand cases involving United States servicemen will be studied and evaluated in the context of how such practice may have been influenced by the mutual defense goals of the countries concerned.

The inquiry will be divided in the following chapters: *(a) Minimum Procedural Safeguards and Customary International Law, (b) Application of SOF "Fair Trial" Safeguards, (c) Denial of "Fair Trial" Safeguards and U.S. Forces, (d) Minimum Standard of Procedural Justice,* and *(e) Summary of Recommendations.*

[35] The term "United States personnel" includes U.S. servicemen, members of the civilian component of the U.S. forces and their dependents who are entitled to the "fair trial" safeguards set out in the various status of forces agreements. In certain parts of this inquiry the term "United States serviceman" is used. Unless otherwise stated members of the civilian component and dependents would be treated similarly to United States servicemen.

[36] See McDougal, "International Law, Power and Policy: A Contemporary Conception, "*Recueil des Cours* (1953), Vol. 1. 140 which identifies the need for a policy-oriented approach to the study of international law.

CHAPTER II

MINIMUM PROCEDURAL SAFEGUARDS AND CUSTOMARY INTERNATIONAL LAW

It is the purpose of this chapter to examine the existing practice of states in order to determine whether or not there is a rule of customary international law which prescribes the procedural safeguards to which an alien is entitled if prosecuted by a host state.

The development of the body of international law pertaining to the responsibility of states for injuries they have caused aliens is probably a classic example of the manner in which community goals, aspirations and policies may affect and reaffect the formulation of international prescriptions.

Although it was recognized by Vattel[1] as early as 1758 that an injury to an alien is an injury to his state,[2] prior to the 19th century there was no well established body of international law pertaining to the responsibility of states for injuries they have caused aliens. In point of fact, in the more or less static world of that time there was comparatively little social and commercial intercourse among nations and, consequently, there was generally no need for such a body of law.[3]

In the 19th and 20th centuries, however, because of the rapid advances made in communication and transportation and because of the great expansion of economic and industrial activity there was a vast increase in commerce and travel among nations, particularly between European nations and those of the new world. During this period the more developed countries of Europe provided technical skill and capital while the less developed countries of the new world provided a source of raw material and a market for manufactured goods.[4] In this rela-

[1] Vattel, *Le Droit des Gens*, Book II, chapter VI.

[2] It should be noted that Vattel was generally considering wrongs inflicted by private individuals upon private individuals.See Dunn, *The Protection of Nationals* (1932) 52 and Parry, "Some Considerations Upon the protection of Individuals in International Law," *Recueil des Cours*, 1956, II, Vol. 90, 42.

[3] Dunn, *op. cit. supra* note 2, at 46.

[4] Jessup, *A Modern Law of Nations* (1948) 95; Fenwick, *International Law* 3d ed. (1948) 275.

tionship, however, the European countries insisted that their nationals be treated by the new countries in generally the same manner as provided in their own legal systems.

In those countries where there was complete dissimilarity in legal systems, the European countries attempted to conduct relationships on a basis of extraterritoriality which in many cases gave them the right to exercise exclusive criminal and civil jurisdiction over their nationals. This was the case in Turkey[5] and certain countries in Eastern Asia.[6] Frequently these demands were made the subject of formal treaties called "Capitulations."[7]

In other less developed countries, such as those in the Western Hemisphere, it was found, that although their legal systems basically reflected European concepts of justice, in practice many of these systems failed to measure up to European standards because of a lack of maturity in their administration. Consequently, clashes inevitably arose between the more developed European states and the less developed states of the new world as to the treatment to be accorded aliens in the latter states.[8] On the part of the European states there were many charges of unjust treatment of their nationals and claims and demands for redress.

During the 19th and 20th centuries these circumstances contributed to the growth of a body of customary international law pertaining to the responsibility of states for injuries to aliens.[9] It is now a principle of customary international law that a host state is responsible to the home state when an alien has suffered injury or damage by an act or omission attributable to the host state, provided that such act or omission is contrary to or wrongful under international law.[10] A state, however, may submit an international claim in behalf of its subjects only when the subject has been unable to obtain redress through the ordinary channels provided by the host state.[11] This has been called the "exhaustion of local remedies" rule, and it represents the point of time at which the home state may present a claim on the international level for injury or damage to its national. This rule was insisted on as

[5] Dunn, *op. cit. supra* note 2, at 54.

[6] *Ibid.*

[7] 1 Oppenheim, *International Law* (8th ed., Lauterpacht 1955) 682; Roth, *The Minimum Standard of International Justice Applied to Aliens*, Leiden 1949, p. 63.

[8] Dunn, *op. cit. supra* note 2, at 54.

[9] Jessup, *op. cit. supra* note 4, at 96.

[10] 1 Oppenheim, *op. cit. supra* note 7, at 336ff.

[11] *Id.* at 361; Schwarzenberger, *International Law*, Vol 1, *International Law as Applied by International Courts and Tribunals:* 1 (3d ed. 1957) 606.

early as the 14th century as a prerequisite before private reprisals would be authorized.[12] The failure to exhaust local remedies, however, will not preclude a claim if it is proved that the utilization of the ordinary channels provided by the host state would not have changed the basis of the complaint.[13]

The principles of state responsibility for injuries to aliens and of the exhaustion of local remedies also have been set out in decisions of the World Court.[14]

In the *Mavrommatis* case[15] the principle of state responsibility for injuries to aliens was expressed as follows:

> It is an elementary principle of international law that a State is entitled to protect its subjects, when injured by acts contrary to international law committed by another State, from whom they have been unable to obtain satisfaction through the ordinary channels. By taking up the case of its subjects and by resorting to diplomatic action or international judicial proceedings on his behalf, a State is in reality asserting its own rights – its right to ensure, in the person of its subjects, respect for the rules of international law... Once a State has taken up a case on behalf of one of its subjects before an international tribunal, in the eyes of the latter the State is sole claimant.

In the *Interhandel* case[16] the local remedies rule was stated as follows:

> The rule that local remedies must be exhausted before international proceedings may be instituted is a well-established rule of customary international law; the rule has been generally observed in cases in which a State has adopted the cause of its national whose rights are claimed to have been disregarded in another State in violation of international law. Before resort may be had to an international court in such a situation, it has been considered necessary that the State where the violation occurred should have an opportunity to redress it by its own means, within the framework of its own domestic legal systems.

The jurisprudence on state responsibility for injuries to aliens has been amplified by the occasional recourse of nations to international arbitration tribunals for the settlement of claims for injuries to aliens. The decisions of these tribunals have provided a source of "case law" for international lawyers.[17] It is notable that this practice began with the

[12] Freeman, *Denial of Justice* (1938) 53–54.
[13] 1 Oppenheim, *op. cit. supra* note 7, at 361.
[14] The term "World Court" is used herein to mean the Permanent Court of International Justice and/or the International Court of Justice.
[15] "Mavrommatis Palestine Concessions Case," *P.C.I.J.* (1924) Series A, No. 2, p. 12.
[16] *Interhandel Case, I.C.J. Reports* (1949) p. 27 (Judgment of March 21st 1959). See also *Panevezys-Saldutiskis Railway Case, P.C.I.J.* (1939) Series A/B, No. 76 where the court sustained a preliminary objection that it did not have jurisdiction of the claim of Estonia against Lithuania until the company whose claims had been espoused by Estonia had exhausted its remedies in the Lithuanian courts.
[17] See Hudson, *International Tribunals Past and Future* (1944) 196 for a survey of the

Jay Treaty of 1795 between the United States and Great Britain which included provisions for the establishment of three arbitration commissions to resolve the St. Croix River boundary dispute, the claims of British subjects for confiscated debts, and certain other reciprocal claims for the seizure of vessels.[18]

Notwithstanding the existence of a rule of customary international law pertaining to state responsibility for injuries to aliens, it should be noted that the effectiveness of the rule as a means of securing redress is severely limited by the following factors:

(1) Discretion of the Alien's State. Under traditional international law individuals are not subjects of international law. Consequently, although an alien may have a right to make a claim against a host state under its municipal law, under international law in the absence of special agreement only his state may submit a claim against the host state. It has been held by the World Court that the state does not merely substitute itself for the individual but rather asserts its own rights.[19] As there is no rule of international law which imposes a duty upon the alien's home state to submit such a claim, a state, unless required otherwise by its domestic law, has discretion as to the submission of such a claim.[20] In this respect the United States has frequently declined to press diplomatic representation in behalf of otherwise meritorious claimants because of some overriding policy designed to foster foreign relations.[21] It also appears probable that other nations have followed the same practice.[22] This uncertainty as to whether a claim will be interposed precludes any effective uniform treatment in

operation of 60 tribunals of a temporary character created to deal with general categories of claims. Hudson points out that despite this practice many states of the world have not participated with other states in such tribunals and that on the whole the creation of such tribunals must be regarded as an exceptional procedure rather than the normal conduct of interstate relations. In this respect the United States had participated in 26 tribunals (19 with ten Latin American states, four with European states, and three with Great Britain); Great Britain has created nine tribunals with eight Latin American states and three with two European states; Venezuela was a party before 14 tribunals; Mexico before eight; France before seven; Colombia before five; Italy and Chile each before four; Belgium, Germany, Panama, and Spain each before three; and the Netherlands and Sweden each before two tribunals. In six incidents both of the interested states were Latin American.

[18] Articles V, VI, and VII of the Treaty of Amity, Commerce and Navigation (Jay Treaty) ratifications exchanged October 28, 1795. Malloy, *Treaties, Conventions, International Acts, Protocols and Agreements between the United States and other Powers 1776–1909*, Vol. 1, p. 590.

[19] *Nottebohm (Second phase) Case, I.C.J. Reports* (1955) 24; *Mavrommatis Palestine Concessions Case, P.C.I.J.* (1924) Series A, No. 2, 12; *Chorzow Factory Case, P.C.I.J.* (1928) Series A, No. 17, 25–29.

[20] 1 Oppenheim, *op. cit. supra* note 7, at 686–7.

[21] Jessup, *op.cit. supra* note 4, at 98.

[22] 1 Oppenheim, *op. cit. supra* note 7, at 687.

this area and may leave the alien without any remedy under international law.

(2) Delay in Obtaining Redress. An examination of the case histories of a number of claims initiated by the United States discloses that there is often from 10 to 20 years between the act or omission upon which the claim is predicated and the payment of reparation.[23]

(3) Self-help. International law during the formulative period of the principle of state responsibility recognized the right of the alien's state to resort to an act of coercion designed to force adequate reparation from the offending state. Notable examples of such armed intervention were the French interventions in Mexico in 1838 and 1861, the intervention of Germany, Great Britain, and Italy in Venezuela in 1902–03, and the interventions of the United States in San Domingo in 1904 and Haiti in 1915. The use of force, however, as a means of coercion in the settlement of disputes among nations is now prohibited by Article 2 of the United Nations Charter.[24] Accordingly, in the absence of submission of the issue to the World Court or any other international arbitration body, it would appear that economic sanctions or world opinion would be the only lawful means for an alien's state to bring pressure upon a host state to make reparation for injuries to the alien.

An examination of the general principle of customary international law pertaining to state responsibility for injuries to aliens discloses that one of the requirements that must be fulfilled before a state may intervene diplomatically in behalf of its subject is that there be an act or omission attributable to the host state which is contrary to or wrongful under international law.

Thus, before a state may incur responsibility for the denial of a procedural safeguard to an alien, it must be established that such a denial is contrary to or wrongful under international law. In this respect, is there any standard which prescribes the procedural safeguards to which an alien is entitled under customary international law?

Conflicting community goals and aspirations on the part of weak and strong states resulted in the decision makers of such states espousing two divergent theories regarding the standard of the procedural safeguards which a host country must accord in the prosecution of an alien.

[23] See e.g. *Chattin Case, United States* v. *Mexico, Opinions of the Commissioners* (1927) 422, where there was a delay of 15 years between the action upon which the claim was predicated and the arbitration thereof and Italy (Gevtini) v. Venezuela, Italy-Venezuela, Mixed Claims Commission, 1903, *Rolston's Reports* 724 where there was a delay of 32 years to arbitration. For further examples of delay see cases set out in *Opinions of the Commissioners, supra.*

[24] *T.S.* 993, June 26, 1945.

On the one hand, the less developed and weaker states, whose legal systems fell below the norms of the more sophisticated and stronger states, insisted that an alien was entitled only to the procedural safeguards accorded by the domestic law of the host state to its own nationals. These states resented and regarded as unwarranted interference the contention of the more developed and stronger states that their nationals engaged in commerce abroad were entitled when prosecuted by a host state to the procedural safeguards set out in a universal minimum standard of justice for all aliens. In practice these safeguards usually comprised the procedural safeguards set out in the domestic law of the home state. These theories are known respectively as the "national treatment" theory and the "minimum standard" theory. Each theory is now supported by a substantial body of "policy-oriented" legal doctrine and rules.

Both of these theories must be examined in order to ascertain whether either of them provides a discernable standard of procedural safeguards which a host state is required by customary international law to accord in the prosecution of an alien.

(1) "National Treatment" Theory

In substance, the "national treatment" theory asserts that an alien is entitled only to those procedural safeguards which are provided to nationals of the host state. It is based on the premise that an alien must accept the legal conditions which he finds in the host country. Consequently, it is maintained that neither the alien nor his government may legitimately complain if he is accorded the same treatment as nationals of the host country. Thus, under this theory a denial of a procedural safeguard would be contrary to or wrongful under international law only if the nationals of the host state would be entitled under its domestic law to such a safeguard.

The "national treatment" theory has derived its main support from Latin American publicists[25] and governments.[26]

[25] Calvo, *Le Droit International* (Paris) 5th ed. 1896, Vol III; Alvarez, *Le Droit International Américain* (Paris) 1910; *Recueil des Cours* Garcìa Amador, "State Responsibility Some New Problems," p. 369, 1958, II (Vol. 94); Fenwick, "Intervention: Individual and Collective," 39 *A.J.I.L.* 645 (1945).

[26] See *International Conferences of American States 1889–1928; International Conferences of American States 1933–1940; Acts of The Conference For The Codification of International Law*, held at The Hague from March 13th to April 12th 1930, Vol. IV, Minutes of the Third Committee, "Responsibility of States For Damages Caused in Their Territory to the Person or Property of Foreigners," *League of Nations Document* No. C 351(C). M. 145 (C), 1930. V.

In this respect García Amador states:[27]

> In the American continent, too, the right of a State to protect its nationals has received general acceptance but in accordance with another principle, the 'principle of equality between nationals and aliens'... The abuses which had occurred in the exercise of diplomatic protection by certain States led, understandably, to a reaction against the very principle which used to be involved as the foundation of the State. The Argentine jurist, Carlos Calvo, referring to this state of affairs, proclaimed the doctrine which has since been pleaded in answer to international claims based on the violation of the 'international standard of justice.' In his opinion, 'aliens who establish themselves in a country are certainly entitled to the same rights of protection as nationals, but they cannot claim any greater measure of protection.'[28]

This theory was indorsed by Latin American States at The First International Conference of the American States (Wash., D. C., 1889–1890) which recommended the adoption of the following rules as principles of American International Law, "(i) Foreigners are entitled to enjoy all the civil rights enjoyed by natives; and they shall be accorded all the benefits of said rights in all that is essential as well as in the form or procedure and the legal remedies incident thereto, absolutely in like manner as said natives (ii) a nation has not, nor recognizes in favor of foreigners, any other obligations or responsibilities than those which in favor of the natives are established, in like cases by the constitution and the laws."[29]

Further, these principles were reaffirmed and included in a subsequent convention on Rights and Duties of States signed at the Seventh International Conference of American States (Montevideo, 1933).[30]

The "national treatment" theory was also placed in issue at the Hague Conference for the Codification of International Law. On 4 April 1930 at the Fifteenth Meeting of the Third Committee which considered the codification of international law pertaining to the *Responsibility of States For Damages Caused in Their Territory to the Person or Property of Foreigners* Dr . C. C. Wu, the Chinese delegate,[31] proposed a single

[27] Amador, *supra* note 25, at 432.

[28] But see Freeman, "Recent Aspects of the Calvo Doctrine and the Challenge to International Law," 40 *A.J.I.L.* 132 et seq. to the effect that Calvo did not go to the extent of maintaining that equality with nationals under local law was in itself a bar to any international inquiry.

[29] *International Conferences of American States 1889–1928, supra* note 26, at 45. The United States delegation submitted a minority report and voted against the recommendation.

[30] *International Conference of American States,* First Supplement 1933–1940 pp. 121–123. This convention was signed by the United States but with a reservation based upon the lack of time to prepare the necessary interpretations and definitions of the proposed doctrines and principles.

[31] *Acts of The Conference For The Codification of International Law, supra* note 26, at 187.

standard for the treatment of aliens; that of the treatment accorded to a nation's own nationals. In support of this proposal Dr. Wu argued that when a person goes to another country he goes there with full knowledge of the conditions, that he knows the conditions in that country as the administration of justice as well as he knows the climatic conditions; that he goes to the foreign country uninvited; that the foreigner should leave if he does not like the country; and that therefore there is no reason why a host Government should "be saddled with a heavier responsibility than which it has towards its own nationals."

The vote[32] by roll call on the proposal of the Chinese delegation was as follows:

For the Proposal: Brazil, Chile, China, Colombia, Czechoslovakia, Free City of Danzig, Egypt, Mexico, Nicaragua, Persia, Poland, Portugal, Roumania, Salvador, Turkey, Uruguay, Yugoslavia.

Against the Proposal: Australia, Austria, Belgium, Canada, Denmark Estonia, Finland, France, Germany, Great Britain, Greece, Hungary, India, Ireland, Italy, Japan, Netherlands, Norway, South Africa, Spain, Sweden, Switzerland, United States of America.

The following abstained: Cuba, Latvia.

Although the "national treatment" proposal of the Chinese delegate was rejected by 23 votes to 17, the roll call demonstrated that a substantial number of states adhered to it. Further, the disagreement between the two groups of nations proved to be so fundamental as to defy compromise, and it has been considered that the proposed convention foundered on this issue.[33]

Additionally, the "national treatment" theory has received support from various arbitration bodies. In this respect it was summarized by the President of the Claims Arbitration Commission between Salvador and the United States of America in the *Rosa Gelbtrunk* claim (1902)[34] as follows:

> A citizen or subject of one nation who, in the pursuit of commercial enterprise, carries on trade within the territory and under the protection of a nation other than his own is to be considered as having cast his lot with the subjects or citizens of the State in which he resides and carries on business ...The State to which he

[32] *Id.* at 188.

[33] See Borchard, "The 'Minimum Standard' of the Treatment of Aliens," Proceedings of *A.J.I.L.* at its 33rd meeting (1939) 55 and Hudson, "The First Conference For the Codification of International Law," 24 *A.J.I.L.* 460 (1930).

[34] *Rosa Gelbtrunk Claim*, 1902, Ralston, *The Law and Procedure of International Tribunals*, 1926, Vol. 1, p. 477; *U.S. Foreign Relations* (1902) 877. See also *Dr. Baldwin's Minatitlan Claims*, (1839) *Moore Arbitrations*, sec. 3238 *et seq.*

owes national allegiance has no right of claim for him as against the nation in which he is resident any other or different treatment... [than] which the latter country metes out to its own subjects or citizens.

An examination of the "national treatment" theory discloses that by treating nationals and aliens alike it restricts the area in which a State may incur responsibility under international law for the operation of its municipal law with respect to aliens. In other words as long as nationals and aliens are similarly treated there is no limitation on the territorial supremacy of the host State. Thus, this theory represents a natural reaction by weaker States against incidents of unjust intervention in their affairs by stronger States.[35]

By equalizing the treatment of national and alien, the "national treatment" theory presents no difficulty in determining the procedural safeguards to which an alien would be entitled if prosecuted by a host State. The norm would simply be the procedural safeguards provided by the municipal law of the host state for its nationals who are similarly prosecuted and there would be an act or omission which is contrary to or wrongful under international law only when such a safeguard is denied to an alien. The safeguards, however, would vary from state to state and might result in some cases in the application of a particularly low standard.

(2) "Minimum Standard" Theory

In substance this theory holds that there is a universal minimum standard of procedural justice according to which all aliens are entitled to be treated. Any denial by the host state of a procedural safeguard prescribed by this standard would by considered contrary to or wrongful under international law. Under this theory, if the treatment of an alien is below the international standard, the host state would not be entitled to the defense that its nationals were similarly treated.

The "minimum standard" theory has been vigoriously advocated by a great number of highly qualified publicists.[36] A statement by Elihu Root which is often quoted in support of this theory is as follows:

[35] Borchard, *The Diplomatic Protection of Citizens Abroad* (1951) 178.

[36] 1 Oppenheim, *op.cit.* note 7, at 350; Freeman, *op. cit.* note 12, at 497–530; Eagelton, *The Responsibility of States* (1928) pp. 82–87; Verdross, *Recueil des Cours*, Vol. 37 (1931 111) 353–357; Scelle, *Revue Générale de Droit International Public, R.G.D.I.P.*, Vol. 34 (1927) 464–465; Dunn, *op. cit.* note 2, at 113–172; Beckett, *Grotius Society*, Vol. 17 (1932) pp. 175–194; Cavaglieri, *Recueil des Cours*, Vol. 26 (1929 I) 456; Fenwick, *op. cit.* note 4, at 279; Fitzmaurice, "The Meaning of the Term Denial of Justice," 13 *B.Y.I.L.* 100–101 (1932); Brierly, *The Law of Nations* 3d ed. 1942 172–174; *Restatement of the Foreign Relations Law of the United States*, The American Law Institute (Tentative Draft No. 5, April 22, 1961) sec. 103, "The Basis of Protection of Citizens Residing Abroad."

> There is a standard of justice, very simple, very fundamental and of such general acceptance by all civilized countries as to form a part of the international law of the world. The condition upon which any country is entitled to measure the justice due from it to an alien by the justice it accords to its own citizens is that its system of law and administration shall conform to this general standard. If any country's system of law and administration does not conform to that standard, although the people of the country may be content or compelled to live under it, no other country can be compelled to accept it as furnishing a satisfactory measure of treatment to its citizens.[37]

The existence of such a minimum standard was also articulated in many of the decisions of the U.S.-Mexican Claims Commission.

In the *Neer* case[38] (1926), one of the first claims considered by the Commission, it was stated:

> The propriety of governmental acts should... be put to the test of international standards. The treatment of an alien, in order to constitute an international delinquency should amount to an outrage, to bad faith, to wilful neglect of duty, or to an insufficiency of governmental action so far short of international standards that every reasonable and impartial man would readily realize its insufficiency. Whether the insufficiency proceeds from the deficient execution of a reasonable law or from the fact that the laws of the country do not empower the authorities to measure up to international standards, is immaterial.

Some of the other Mexican Claims Commission cases which affirmed the existence of a minimum standard of treatment were the Faulkner Claim,[39] the Harry Roberts claim,[40] the Chase claim,[41] and the Hopkins claim.[42]

The existence of a minimum standard of international law with respect to the protection of foreign property was expressly recognized in dicta of the Permanent Court of Arbitration in the Norwegian Shipowners' claims (1922) when the court declared the discriminatory treatment of the property rights of citizens and foreigners to be contrary to the municipal law of the United States and also to international law.[43]

Finally, the "minimum standard" theory has been vigorously advanced by the United States in protest of the treatment of its na-

[37] American Society of International Law, *Proceedings*, 1910 pp. 20–21.

[38] *U.S.A. (L. F. Neer)* v. *United Mexican States*, Opinions of Comm'rs (1926), 71.

[39] *U.S.A. (W. H. Faulkner)* v. *United Mexican States*, Opinions of Comm'rs (1927) 86.

[40] *U.S.A. (Harry Roberts)* v. *United Mexican States*, Opinions of Comm'rs (1927) 100.

[41] *U.S.A. (John D. Chase)* v. *United Mexican States*, Opinion of Comm'rs (1929) 17.

[42] *U.S.A. (George W. Hopkins)* v. *United Mexican States*, Opinions of Comm'rs (1927) 42.

[43] 1 *U.N. Rep. Int'l Arb. Awards* 219 (1922). As to other decisions of the Permanent Court of Arbitration dealing with the minimum standard and the protection of foreign property see Canevaro (1912) 1 Scott 290; French Claims Against Peru 1 *U.N. Rep. Int'l Arb. Awards* 219 (1921).

tionals by foreign governments. An example of this was the statement of Acting Secretary Polk to the Mexican Government (1918) that:

> The Government of the United States is firmly of the opinion that the great weight of international law and practice supports the view that every nation has certain minimum duties to perform with regard to the treatment of foreigners, irrespective of its duties to its own citizens, and that in default of such performance, it is the right of the foreign government concerned to enter protest.[44]

Examination of the "minimum standard" theory shows that it imposes certain limitations on the territorial supremacy of a state with respect to the procedural safeguards it must accord aliens. Thus, under this theory an alien could be entitled to more procedural safeguards than a national if the municipal law of the host country is below the minimum standard.

What, however, are the procedural safeguards prescribed by the minimum standard?

Unfortunately the vagueness of the standard makes any *a priori* determination of its content a hopeless task.

This lack of precision has been sharply criticized by Professor Dunn who stated:

> ...the efforts of the authorities to give specific content to this 'very simple, very fundamental' standard have resulted in the utmost confusion and vagueness.[45]

Further, such leading proponents of the minimum standard theory as Borchard,[46] Freeman,[47] and Eagleton[48] have also admitted its imperfection as a definitive norm.

Since an *a priori* attempt to define the content of the minimum standard is not possible, can a definition be formulated by empirical means; that is, by an examination of the existing practice of states?

An examination of international practice as to the minimum procedural safeguards to be accorded an alien prosecuted by a host state

[44] Mr. Polk, Acting Secretary to Ambassador Henry P. Fletcher, Dec. 13, 1918, *Foreign Relations of the United States 1918*, 786–787; See also Note of Secretary Hull to Mexico, Aug. 22, 1938, Supplement to 32 *A.J.I.L.*, 191 (1938).

[45] Dunn, *op. cit. supra* note 2, at 144. See also Amador, *supra* note 25, at 436.

[46] Borchard, *Annuaire de l'Institut de Droit International* (1931) 55 in which he states the standard is "vague, deceiving and confused properly calculated to produce error, for it pretends to express a conception which in reality seldom if ever exists."

[47] Freeman, *op. cit. supra* note 12, at 546–7.

[48] Eagleton, *op. cit. supra* note 36, at 109 where he states that the indefiniteness of the standard leaves small states at the mercy of larger ones in the matter of such claims but it has compensatory value in exerting an influence toward a uniform protection of the individual throughout the world.

discloses that an unreasonable delay in trial,[49] lack of opportunity to cross-examine,[50] failure to be informed of the charges and lack of knowledge of the testimony of the prosecution's witnesses,[51] refusal to allow the presentation of a defense,[52] refusal to allow defense counsel,[53] not informing a defendant of the charges against him,[54] and refusal to furnish an interpreter[55] have all been held to constitute violations of the standard.

Further examination, however, discloses that the vast majority of these and similar instances are from United States diplomatic practice or from cases decided by the United States-Mexican Claims Tribunals.[56] It thus can scarcely be maintained that they are representative of the existing practice of states.

Accordingly, it must be concluded that a paramount difficulty in the application of the minimum standard is that its content is not susceptible of definition.

The foregoing examination of the national treatment theory and the minimum standard theory discloses that a substantial number of states and publicists have adhered to each theory. In this respect the closeness of the vote (23–17) on Dr. Wu's proposal for national treatment at the Hague Codification Conference[57] demonstrates that numerically the nations involved were almost evenly divided. Further, it may be expected that many of the nations in Africa and Asia who have recently acquired their independence, as well as the Soviet Bloc countries, will be in favor of the national treatment theory since it infringes the least on their territorial supremacy.

In view of this dichotomy, it cannot be said that there is evidence of a constant and uniform practice upon which could be predicated the positive requirements of a rule of customary international law with respect to the procedural safeguards to be accorded an alien prosecuted by a host state.[58]

[49] Mr. Bayard, Secretary of State to Mr. Jackson, July 26, 1886, For. Rel. 1882, 6 *Moore's Dig.* 281.

[50] *Ibid.*

[51] 5 Hackworth, *Digest of International Law*, 545.

[52] Mr. Conrad, Acting Secretary of State, to Mr. Peyton, Oct. 12, 1852, 2 Wharton 613, 6 *Moore's Dig.* 274.

[53] *C. W. Parrish* (*U.S.* v. *Mexico*), Opinions of Comm'rs (1927) 473, 482.

[54] Mr. Frelinghuyser, Secretary of State to Mr. Lowell, Minister to England, April 25, 1882, For. Rel. 1882, 6 *Moore's Dig.* 275.

[55] Freeman, *op. cit. supra* note 12, at 278.

[56] See cases cited in Supplement to *A.J.I.L.* Vol. 23 (1929) p. 173 *et seq.* and in Freeman, *op. cit. supra* note 12, at 273 et seq.

[57] *Acts of the Conference For the Codification of International Law, supra* note 20, at 188. It is recognized of course, that these votes are not binding on the states concerned.

[58] See the *Asylum Case, I.C.J. Reports* (1950) 276 and *Rights of U.S. Nationals, I.C.J. Reports* (1952) 200 which set out the criteria for customary international law.

The most that can be claimed from the practice of states on this subject is that there exists a regional rule of customary international law in the Latin-American states as to the national treatment theory. In this respect there appears to be among those states a constant and uniform observance of the national treatment theory accompanied by *opininio juris sive necessitatis* in the traditional meaning of this term.[59] This regional rule of customary international law has in turn been set out in conventional international law by these states.[60]

Thus, there is no rule of customary international law which establishes the minimum procedural safeguards to which an alien is entitled if prosecuted by the host state, although there may be a regional custom to that effect in Latin America.

Accordingly, notwithstanding the existence of a general principle of customary international law pertaining to state responsibility when an alien has suffered injury or damage by an act or omission attributable to a state which is contrary to or wrongful under international law, the home state of an alien can not demonstrate that a denial of any procedural safeguard by a host state to an alien was contrary to or wrongful under international law.

This is not to say that a state may not through diplomatic intercourse urge the validity of either the "national treatment" theory or the "minimum standard" theory in cases where its nationals have been injured or damaged. For example, the United States has consistently advocated the "minimum standard" theory. A recent example of the United States position was contained in a note delivered to the Soviet Foreign Office by the American Embassy, Moscow, dated October 6, 1949, which indicated that detention without prompt notice of reason for arrest and information as to charges is wrongful under international law, and is a violation of the minimum standards of justice.[61]

It is to say, however, that there is no principle of customary international law which recognizes either the "national treatment" theory or the "minimum standard" theory.

[59] See *Asylum Case, supra* 276 which laid down the requirements for a regional custom.
[60] See note 26, *supra*.
[61] 21 *Dept State Bull.* 592 (1949).

CHAPTER III

APPLICATION OF SOF 'FAIR TRIAL' SAFEGUARDS

The inclusion of explicit "fair trial" safeguards in the 13 nation NATO SOF Agreement and in 7 bilateral status of forces agreements is a tacit, but massive, recognition by the United States and the other states concerned of the truth of the conclusion of Chapter II; that *customary* international law contains no demonstrable standards, no reliable criteria, for determination of what are the minimal procedural safeguards international law is said to require host states to accord aliens.

Since the ratification of the NATO SOF Agreement by the United States on July 25, 1953, there have been over 30,000 cases involving United States servicemen, civilian employees of the armed forces, and their dependents over which NATO countries, whose legal systems are different in whole or in part from that of the United States, had the primary right to exercise criminal jurisdiction under the formula set out in paragraph 3 of Article VII, of the agreement.[1] Of this number over 4,000 cases were actually tried by such foreign countries.[2] As each accused so tried was entitled to the procedural safeguards set out in paragraph 9 of Article VII of the NATO SOF Agreement, major differences as to the application and meaning of these safeguards could have arisen between the United States and these countries.

The purpose of this chapter is to determine whether any such differences of interpretation, in fact, have arisen from the day-to-day ap-

[1] See Senate Report No. 1041, 87th Congress, 1st Session, Sept 15, 1961, on the Operation of Article VII, NATO Status of Forces Treaty, 8. The remaining cases were in NATO countries which have a common law system of jurisprudence. In this respect 16,953 cases were subject to the primary jurisdiction of these countries as follows: United Kingdom 13,966, Canada 2,987. The United Kingdom tried 11,300 of these cases while Canada tried 2,528.

[2] *Ibid.*, these trials may be broken down among these countries as follows: Belgium 17, Denmark 1, France 3,100, Greece 6, Italy 515, Luxembourg 150, The Netherlands 2, Norway 21, Portugal 0, and Turkey 203. In the other cases states waived their primary right to exercise jurisdiction to the United States at its request. See par 3(c) of Article VII, NATO SOF Agreement which requires that "sympathetic consideration" be given to such requests.

plication of these safeguards in the prosecution of these thousands of United States servicemen under legal systems different from the United States and, if so, whether the United States and the country concerned have been able to accommodate such differences. It is proposed to isolate any common denominator as to the meaning of these safeguards which may have been agreed upon by the United States and those countries having different systems of law, or, conversely, to isolate any points of disagreement as to the meaning of these safeguards. This analysis will be largely empirical and will be evaluated in the context of how the mutual defense goals and community interests of the countries concerned may have influenced their interpretation of the "fair trial" safeguards. Technical doctrine and rules will not be considered alone, divorced from power and social processes. The body of cases chosen for this analysis is those tried by NATO countries having different systems of law than the United States.

In the United States at the time of the ratification of the NATO SOF Agreement (July 25, 1953) grave doubt was expressed by domestic critics that United States servicemen would receive a fair trial in foreign courts whose systems of law were different from that of the United States.[3] The Senate Foreign Relations Committee, however, was assured by Attorney General Brownell that the "procedural safeguards" contained in paragraph 9 of Article VII of the NATO SOF Agreement were in accordance with "civilized standards of justice" and could be relied upon to insure a "fair trial" to any United States serviceman prosecuted under this Agreement.[4]

The United States Senate recognized the importance of these "fair trial" safeguards to the individual serviceman when it included a paragraph in its resolution of advice and consent to the ratification of the NATO SOF Agreement which directs that any failure on the part of a receiving state to accord these procedural safeguards to a United States serviceman shall be reported to the Commanding Officer of the Armed Forces of the United States in such state who shall then request the Department of State to take appropriate action to protect the rights of the serviceman and notification shall be given by the Executive Branch to the Armed Services Committees of the Senate and House of Representatives.[5]

[3] See statement of Senator Bricker of Ohio, Supplementary Hearings Before the Committee on Foreign Relations United States Senate, 83rd Cong., Ist. Sess., On Status of Forces of the North Atlantic Treaty (June 24, 1953).

[4] *Id.*, at 68.

[5] *T.I.A.S.* 2846, p. 36. See Appendix 1.

The Department of Defense directive setting forth the policy pertaining to the trials of United States Defense personnel by foreign tribunals requires that a United States observer attend all such trials. In the case of minor offenses, however, the attendance of an observer is at the discretion of the designated Commanding Officer.[6] Although these observers must be lawyers, in the case of a minor offense this requirement may be waived.[7] Further, such observers must prepare a formal report on all trials of United States Defense personnel by foreign tribunals which are not for minor offenses.[8] Minor offenses are negatively defined as those which do not involve serious personal injury or extensive property damage or which do not normally result in sentences to confinement.[9]

The directives of the three services which implement the Department of Defense directive establish a format for the trial observer's report.[10] This format includes, *inter alia*, the offense charged, foreign statutes alleged to have been violated, a resume of the proceedings, and comments as to whether all of the "fair trial" safeguards set out in the various SOF agreements have been accorded the accused.[11]

All observer reports are closely scrutinized in turn by both the designated commanding officer in the field and by The Judge Advocate General of the accused's service with a view toward determining whether there has been a denial by the host country of any of the "fair trial" safeguards contained in the various SOF agreements or whether anything has taken place during the trial or appellate procedures which may have caused the trial of the accused to be unfair.

With respect to the heavy demands placed upon the three services in furnishing observers for several thousand trials annually, supervising their activities, and otherwise administering the various SOF agreements, it has been reported to a Sub-Committee of the Senate Committee on Armed Forces by a spokesman for the Department of Defense[12] that-

[6] Section IV, G, 2, Department of Defense Directive Number 5525.1, May 5, 1962, subject: Status of Forces Policies and Information.

[7] Section IV, G, 1, Department of Defense Directive 5525.1, May 5, 1962, subject: Status of Forces Policies and Information.

[8] Section IV, G, 2, Department of Defense Directive Number 5525.1, May 5, 1962, subject: Status of Forces Policies and Information.

[9] Section IV, G, 1, Department of Defense Directive Number 5525.1, May 5, 1962, subject: Status of Forces Policies and Information.

[10] See e.g. Department of the Army letter, AGAM.P(M) 250.3 (10 March 1958), JAGW, subject: "Procedures to be Followed Where United States Personnel are Subject to Foreign Criminal Jurisdiction or Confined in Foreign Penal Institutions," dated 8 April 1958.

[11] A copy of this format is set out at Appendix 2.

[12] Hearings Before a Subcommittee of the Committee on Armed Services, United

The problems are enormous and the problem of criminal jurisdiction in particular is one which demands the constant vigilance of every troop commander and of every staff officer concerned with the administration of the status-of-forces and related agreements.

During recent years, there has been something akin to an administrative revolution in the work of the Defense Department concerned with this problem – whereas, formerly their business was entirely that of administering the Uniform Code of Military Justice, now perhaps one-half of the man-hours of the service personnel abroad in the Judge Advocate General's Corps is devoted to administration of the status of forces agreements.

There has been in effect a conversion from military justice administration to status-of-forces administration. An official American observer attends every trial abroad of which the American authorities have notice.

It is now proposed to examine *seriatim* each of the procedural safeguards set out in paragraph 9 of Article VII of the NATO SOF Agreement with a view toward ascertaining whether any major differences of interpretation have arisen as to their application between the United States and those NATO countries having different systems of law from that of the United States in the trials of over 4,000 United States servicemen by such countries.[13]

(1) The right to a prompt and speedy trial (par 9(a) of Art. VII)

There are three separate elements included in this safeguard. First, that there be a trial rather than punishment inflicted by a bill of attainder or other legislative or executive fiat; second, that the trial be prompt; and, third, that the trial be speedy.

There have been no problems with respect to the accused's right to a trial as the law of all of the civil law countries which are signatory to the NATO SOF Agreement provide for a trial for a criminal offense.[14]

With respect to what constitutes a prompt trial and a speedy trial consider the following two hypothetical situations:

States Senate, On the Operation of Article VII, NATO Status of Forces Treaty, 85th Cong., 2d Sess. (29 July 1958) 2.

[13] This chapter is not concerned with other problems arising from Article VII of the Agreement, such as the interpretation of the criminal jurisdictional formula set out in par 3 of Art. VII. For a discussion of this and other problems arising under this article see Ellert, "The United States as a Receiving State," 63 *Dickinson Law Review* 75; Levie, "Some Legal Problems Arising Under the NATO Status of Forces Agreement and the Administrative Agreement with Japan," 17 *Federal Bar Journal* 620 (1957); Schuck, "Concurrent Jurisdiction Under the NATO Status of Forces Agreement," 57 *Columbia Law Review* 355 (1957), and "Criminal Jurisdiction Over American Armed Forces Abroad," 70 *Harvard Law Review* 1043, April 1957.

[14] See e.g. Belgium, Constitution (Feb. 7, 1931, as amended) Arts. 7, 8, 9, 97, 98;

(1) A United States soldier in Italy is accused of murder of an Italian national for which the maximum punishment under Italian law is more than 20 years' imprisonment; a compulsory warrant of arrest is issued, and he is imprisoned in pre-trial confinement. After one and a half years of imprisonment a verdict of indictment has not been rendered. In this respect Article 272 of the Italian Procedural Code provides that:

> 1. In cases of formal examination ('istruzione formale') a defendant shall be released if a verdict of indictment has not been rendered:
> (a) after two years of imprisonment, if the warrant of arrest is compulsory in connection with the crime and the maximum punishment is not less than 20 years,...

The commanding officer of the accused reports that in his opinion the long pretrial confinement of the accused is unwarranted by the facts of the case and constitutes a denial of the right *to a prompt trial* which is set out in paragraph 9(a) of Article VII, *supra*.

(2) A United States soldier is tried in a civil law country, such as Turkey whose law permits a trial composed of numerous short intermittent hearings over a long period of time. The trial starts on 1 January 1958 and on 1 June 1959 after 26 hearings is still not finished. The United States trial observer reports that in his opinion the Turkish authorities have been dilatory in conducting the trial and that there has been a denial of the right of the serviceman *to a speedy trial* under paragraph 9(a) of Article VII of the Agreement.

The two hypothetical situations illustrate situations which although perfectly consistent with local law in the respective host states are deemed by the local United States commander to be unduly protracted. These cases present the question of what is meant by the words "prompt and speedy trial" as used in paragraph 9(a) of Article VII, *supra*.

Unfortunately, the *travaux préparatoires* of the NATO SOF Agreement are silent as to what constitutes a prompt and speedy trial. Further, there is no customary rule of international law which even accords an alien in a host state the right to a prompt and speedy trial, much less defines its content.[15]

France, *Declaration of Rights of Man and of the Citizen* of August 26, 1789, which is reaffirmed in the Preamble and Art. 66 of the new French Constitution which was adopted by Referendum on 28 Sept. 1958 and promulgated on 4 Oct. 1958; Greece, Constitution (Jan. 1, 1952), Arts. 4, 5; Italy, Constitution (Dec. 22, 1947), Arts. 13, 24, 27, 102, 134; Luxembourg, Constitution (Oct. 17, 1868, as amended), Arts. 12, 13, 14, and Code Penal, Art. 2; Norway Constitution (May 17, 1814, as amended), Arts. 96, 97; Portugal, Constitution (Aug. 1, 1935), Art. 8; Turkey, Constitution (9 July 1961), Art. 33.

[15] See the conclusions of Chapter II.

In the absence of the establishment of any criteria as to what constitutes a prompt and speedy trial it is arguable that this safeguard contemplates a trial which is "prompt and speedy" within the framework for conducting criminal proceedings which has been provided by the receiving state; however, any undue delay by the authorities of the receiving state in complying with such procedures would be a denial of the right to a "prompt and speedy trial" within the meaning of this safeguard.

This interpretation is in accord with decisions of the United States Supreme Court in determining what constitutes a speedy trial under the Sixth Amendment of the Constitution which have generally held that this right is necessarily relative and depends upon the circumstances of each case.[16]

On the other hand regardless of compliance with local law it is also arguable that, as the primary purpose of the NATO SOF Agreement is to support the mutual defense goals of the North Atlantic Treaty Organization,[17] a trial of a member of a sending state's force is not "prompt and speedy" within the meaning of paragraph 9(a) of Article VII, *supra,* if it is so protracted that it interferes with the functional operation of the forces of the sending state.

The latter argument has been advanced in substance by local United States military authorities who have urged foreign authorities to speed up their judicial processes in cases where trial proceedings appear to be unduly drawn out.[18] One major reason for this argument is that under United States statutory law the military authorities may not retain a serviceman in the service beyond the expiration of his term of service unless he volunteers to extend, is turned over to the custody of foreign authorities, or court-martial charges are preferred. Further, protracted trials by foreign authorities severely limit the utilization of the serviceman in his duties, interfere with the duration of his normal overseas service tour, and tend to lower morale.

In general foreign authorities have recognized that lengthy trials of United States servicemen may interfere with the functional operation of the forces of the sending state and have been sympathetic to requests that their judicial processes be accelerated. An illustration of this cooperation is a circular of the French Ministry of Justice to all procurators which emphasizes that there should be "maximum acceleration

[16] *Beavers* v. *Haubert,* 198 U.S. 77, 87 (1905); *Pollard* v. *United States* 352 U.S. 354 (1957).

[17] See Arts. 3 and 4, *T.I.A.S.* 1964, August 24, 1949.

[18] See Report, *op. cit. supra* note 1, at 2.

of proceedings by every available means" in those cases where prosecution would "delay the repatriation" of the United States serviceman or "delay his discharge."[19]

Because of this cooperation on the part of foreign authorities and the recognition by United States authorities that the judicial process in civil law countries is generally more lengthy than in the United States, there have been no major problems with this safeguard. In a recent hearing before a Subcommittee of the Committee on Armed Services, United States Senate, Turkey was reported as the only country where the United States is experiencing difficulty with lengthy trials.[20]

Thus, there is no precise answer to the problems raised in the two hypothetical cases as to what constitutes a "prompt and speedy" trial under the NATO SOF agreement. Eight years of practice, however, disclose that although the United States would probably recognize that the law of the receiving state may determine what constitutes a "prompt and speedy" trial, the authorities of receiving states have in turn recognized the argument of the United States that a trial should not be so protracted as to interfere with the functional operation of the forces of the sending state.

(2) The right to be informed in advance of trial, of the specific charge or charges made against him (par 9(b) of Art. VII)

The procedures of all civil law countries which are signatory to the NATO SOF Agreement provide for notice to the accused well in advance of trial of the specific charge or charges made against him.[21]

[19] Section VI of French Ministry of Justice Circular 58–16, April 9, 1958 states in pertinent part:

> Article VII, 9 of the Agreement provides certain guarantees to the member of the forces, the civilian component and dependents prosecuted in the courts of a receiving State.
>
> It is provided in particular (sub-paragraph a) that the accused has the right to a *prompt and speedy trial.* This provision is in conformity at one and the same time with the good administration of justice, the interests of the Army of which the accused is a member, since it cannot freely dispose of him while the prosecution is pending, and the good reputation abroad of French justice. Particularly in those cases where the prosecution would delay the repatriation of the person concerned, and even more so if it would delay his discharge, the maximum acceleration of the proceedings by every available measure must be insured.

[20] See Hearings on the Operation of Article VII, NATO Status of Forces Treaty, 86th Cong., 2d Sess., June 8, 1960, 8.

[21] See e.g. Belgium, Code d'Instruction Criminelle, Arts. 153, 189, 231; Denmark, Code of Procedure, Secs. 768, 774, 831; Federal Republic of Germany, Code of Criminal Procedure, Sec. 134; France, Code de Procédure Pénale, Arts 114, 197, 214, 215, 217, 268, 279; Italy, Procedural Penal Code, Arts. 264, 376, 395, 396, 398, and 412; Luxem-

There have not as yet been any reports of a violation of this right nor have there been any difficulties in practice with regard to it. Even in those countries, such as Turkey, whose law provides for crimes *flagrante delicto*, where the accused is immediately brought before a court for a hearing, there have not been any reports of United States servicemen being denied this right.

In theory, however, there exists in some civil law countries a potential source of difficulty.

Consider the hypothetica lcase of a soldier who is tried and convicted by the Yokohama District Court for wounding through robbery in violation of Article 240 of the Japanese Penal Code. The accused appeals his case to the Tokyo High Court and at this time the prosecutor introduces a new charge, conspiracy to embezzle money, in violation of Articles 252 and 253 of the Japanese Penal Code, which is based on evidence introduced by the accused at the trial level. Under Japanese law this is not a lesser included offense of robbery. Subsequently, the appellate court sets aside the robbery charge and finds the accused guilty of the newly added charge of conspiracy to embezzle money. The United States trial observer reports that he feels that this is a violation of paragraph 9(b) of Article XVII of the Japanese Administrative Agreement[22] which is identical with paragraph 9(b) of Article VII of the NATO SOF Agreement, as the accused did not have notice in advance of trial of the added charge.

On first examination the contention of the trial observer appears to have some validity, especially when examined in the light of Anglo-American common law jurisprudence wherein the function of appellate proceedings is essentially to review what took place at the trial level. Intermediate appellate proceedings in civil law countries, however, are on both the law and facts and are really trials *de novo*. Inasmuch as the Japanese Code provides that the accused must be informed in advance of the appellate proceedings of the new charge, he received the advance notice required by this safeguard. Consequently, there would be no basis in the hypothetical case for a protest by the United States that the accused was denied advance notice of the charge against him. In such cases, however, where there is an absence of advance notice of the new charge, there would appear to be a denial of this safeguard.

bourg, Code d'Instruction Criminelle, Art. 93; The Netherlands, Code of Criminal Procedure, Art. 258; Turkey, Code of Criminal Procedure, Art. 106. In Iceland the Annex to the Defense Agreement (T.I.A.S. 2295) which contains the "fair trial" safeguards set out in par 9 of Art. VII of the NATO SOF Agreement has become part of Icelandic statutory law (No. 110/1951).

(3) The right to be confronted with the witnesses against him (par 9(c) of Art. VII)

The underlying difficulty that the United States has experienced with this safeguard is with the meaning of the word "confronted".

Consider the case of a United States soldier who is tried for rape in a French court. The prosecutrix is called into the hearing and the president of the court asks her to repeat her statement in the presence of the accused. Counsel for the accused desires to cross-examine the prosecutrix and is told that he must submit his questions to the president who is the only one who may question the witness. The United States trial observer reports that this is not a fair trial as the accused had not had the opportunity to test the credibility of the prosecutrix by cross-examination which under United States law is included in the right of confrontation.

In the civil law countries confrontation ordinarily consists of calling a witness into the hearing and requiring him to repeat his statement in the presence of the accused.[23] Neither the prosecution nor the defense has the right to cross-examine witnesses, but they do have the right to request the judge in his discretion to put particular questions to a witness. Its efficacy depends on the psychological fact that a hostile witness is less likely to testify falsely if he is required to give his testimony in the presence of the person against whom he is testifying.

On the other hand under United States constitutional law the purpose of the right of the accused to be confronted with the witnesses against him[24] was to preserve a common law right of confrontation which had certain recognized exceptions.[25] For example, the Sixth Amendment does not preclude the admission of a dying declaration,[26] nor of the stenographic report of testimony given at a former trial by a witness since deceased.[27] In this respect Dean Wigmore has emphasized that

[22] Agreement under Article VI of the Treaty of Mutual Cooperation and Security Between the United States of America and Japan, signed at Washington on Jan. 19, 1960 (*T.I.A.S.* 4510).

[23] See e.g. France, Code de Procédure Penale, 323–338; Italy, Code of Criminal Procedure, Art. 212; Turkey, Code of Civil Procedure, Chapter 6, Arts. 250 *et seq.*; Luxembourg, Code d'Instruction Criminelle, Arts. 153, 190; in Denmark and Norway the examination of witnesses is conducted by the prosecutor and defense counsel. See Denmark, Code of Procedure, Secs. 172, 180, and 872; see Williams, The Proof of Guilt 28–32 (1955) for a comparison of the civil and common law method of examination of witnesses.

[24] United States Constitution, Amend. VI.

[25] *Salinger* v. *United States*, 272 U.S. 542, 548 (1926).

[26] *Kirby* v. *United States*, 174 U.S. 47, 61 (1809); *Robertson* v. *Baldwin*, 165 U.S. 275, 282 (1897).

[27] *Mattox* v. *United States*, 156 U.S. 237, 240 (1895).

in the common law there never was any recognized right to an indispensable thing called confrontation as distinguished from cross-examination; there was, however, a right to cross-examine which was indispensable and which was secured by confrontation.[28]

This difference as to the meaning of confrontation between the civil law countries and the common law countries is, of course, inherent in their respective systems of jurisprudence. The common law system is primarily adversary in nature. Opposing counsel dominate the proceedings and judges have an essentially arbitral function. Consequently, an essential part of this system is the right to cross-examine and this is the primary objective of confrontation. In the civil law system the judge actually directs the trial and controls the evidence, and the parties to the trial play a supplementary and subsidiary part. The civil law judge is familiar with a case before the main trial, and cross-examination by counsel is not an essential element of confrontation.[29]

An examination of the *travaux préparatoires* of the NATO SOF Agreement does not disclose that the drafters of the Agreement intended to attach any particular meaning to the words "to be confronted" which are contained in this safeguard. It would appear that if the drafters had intended to modify what has been a long established practice in civil law countries they would have specifically set forth this modification. Accordingly, it must be concluded that the words "to be confronted" are to be subjectively interpreted in accordance with the legal system of the receiving state. As the accused in the hypothetical case has been provided the form of confrontation provided by French law, there is no ground upon which the United States may protest that this type of confrontation is a violation of this fair trial standard because it does not permit cross-examination by the accused.

An early case under the Agreement which illustrates another aspect

[28] *Wigmore Evidence*, 3d ed., sec. 1397 (1940).

[29] International proceedings have illustrated that these differences in the common and civil law systems are far from being unbridgeable. The World Court has had little difficulty in blending civil and common law principles of procedure. This was also successfully accomplished in the Nuremburg trials of leading war criminals. See W. H. Friedman, *Legal Theory*, 369 (3d ed. 1953). Further, although civil law systems do not contain direct or cross-examination as known in the common law, such systems do contain inducements for eliciting the truth from a witness. For example, in France, if it appears from the hearing that the testimony of a witness is false, the President of the Court of Assizes may, on his own, or on request from the public prosecutor or one of the parties, order the said witness to be present at the hearing until its termination and to remain in the hearing room until the decision of the court, at which time he may order that the witness shall be taken by the police to the Procureur de la Republique for an investigation (Art. 342, C.P.P.). Parallel provisions are applicable to trials before the Tribunal Correctionnel and the Tribunal de Police (Art. 454, 457, 536, C.P.P.).

of the confrontation problem in civil law countries is the *Baldwin* case. This case arose in France and was the first one in which the full formal procedure called for by the Senate resolution was invoked.

On 7 October 1953 PFC Jerry Baldwin, U.S. Army, was found guilty by a French court of an assault upon a French national and sentenced to pay a fine of 6,000 francs ($18.00). During the trial the accused was not confronted with the witnesses against him. Although this was proper under French law, United States authorities protested to the French authorities that Baldwin had not been confronted with the witnesses against him as required by paragraph 9, Article VII of the NATO SOFA. The Ministry of Justice agreed with the United States view and directed that the sentence of the court be appealed by the Procureur General. Although that official was informed of the reason for the appeal, the Cour d'Appel, Orleans, which heard the appeal on 25 March 1954 was not informed of it. Consequently, that court assuming that the appeal had been ordered because the sentence was inadequate affirmed the lower court's conviction and increased the fine to 12,000 francs ($36.00). At this appeal, as in the lower court, no witnesses appeared and the trial was by means of a case file. As the appellate court had merely compounded the error committed by the lower court a new protest was made to the French Ministry of Justice through the United States Embassy in Paris. The Ministry of Justice then remitted the fine against Baldwin, and instructed the Procureur-General to insure the avoidance of similar errors in the future. Private Baldwin desired no further appeal to be taken in his case.[30]

It thus appears that France recognized the validity of the United States position that the confrontation required by Article VII, paragraph 9(c) *supra*, clearly requires the accused to be physically present when an adverse witness testifies against him even though French domestic law permits the contrary. In other civil law countries it has generally been the practice to call all adverse witnesses to testify before a trial court when a United States serviceman is being tried.[31]

[30] A full statement of the facts of this case is set out in the Hearings Before a Subcommittee of the Committee on Armed Services, United States Senate, 84th Cong., 1st sess., on the Operation of Article VII, NATO Status of Forces Treaty, March 29, 31, and June 21, 1955, 21–23. Section VI, French Ministry of Justice Circular 58–16, April 9, 1958 states in this respect: "subparagraph c [par. 9c, Art. VII, NATO SOF A] specifies that the accused is entitled *to be confronted with the witnesses against him*. The authorities of the states where the rules of Anglo-Saxon procedure are in effect place a great deal of importance on compliance with this rule."

[31] The basis of this statement is an examination of observer reports pertaining to the trial of United States servicemen on file in the Offices of the Judge Advocates General of the Army, Navy, and Air Force.

There was also reported to the Sub-Committee of the Committee on Armed Forces, United States Senate, several cases which arose in France involving these two situations: First, where, although there was no confrontation at the original trial, confrontation was afforded at the appellate level,[32] and second, where there was no confrontation at the trial but the accused did not desire an appeal to be taken in his behalf.[33] It was decided by the Sub-Committee that these situations were not to be reported under paragraph 4 of the Senate Resolution as a violation of paragraph 9(c) of Article VII of the NATO SOFA.[34]

The confrontation problem has been further complicated by civil law practice of conducting trials *in absentia*.[35] Under civil law there exists a procedure whereby a person who has committed an offense under local law and who has left the country may by a form of substituted service by mail to the last known address of the individual or his present address in the country where he is residing be tried *in absentia*. Thus, United States personnel in such countries might be tried after their departure from the territory of the receiving state.

In practice *in absentia* trials usually arise in this fashion: There is notice by the receiving state to the accused or to the sending state while the accused is in the receiving state of the commission of an offense in violation of local law. Under United States law if the enlistment or term of military service of the accused is due to expire, military authorities have no legal right to hold the accused beyond that date unless he consents thereto or he is charged with an offense and confined by the authorities of the receiving state.[36] In such cases where the receiving state authorities do not desire to confine the accused, and the accused after a full explanation of his rights consents to be tried *in absentia* and the authorities of the receiving state also consent to this procedure, the accused may be returned to the United States and tried by the receiving state *in absentia*.[37]

The United States has not protested that an *in absentia* trial under these circumstances is a violation of the right to confrontation under

[32] Hearings, *op. cit. supra* note 30, at 23, 58, 59.

[33] *Ibid.*

[34] *Ibid.*

[35] See e.g. Codice de Procedura Penale (Italy), Arts. 447–450; Code de Procédure Pénale (France, Arts. 627–641).

[36] Another alternative to retain an enlisted man in the service beyond the term of his enlistment is to prefer court-martial charges (par. 11d, Manual for Courts Martial 1951).

[37] See letter to Commander in Chief, United States Army, Europe, from Department of the Army, subject: "Trials in Absentia of United States Personnel," dated 24 April 1959, as to policy on this subject.

the NATO SOFA. The reasoning for this position is apparently that paragraph 9, Article VII of the NATO SOFA provides only that the accused *shall be entitled* to be confronted with the witnesses against him and not that the accused can be tried only if he can be confronted with the witnesses against him. Thus, it is argued that, if the foreign government provides the opportunity for confrontation at the trial and the accused voluntarily chooses not to appear at the trial, there has been an effective waiver by the accused of his right to confrontation. Consequently, neither he nor his government is in a position to contend that the right has been denied.[38]

In those cases, however, where an *in absentia* trial is held by the receiving state without the consent of the accused, the United States authorities would undoubtedly consider this to be a violation of the right to confrontation under paragraph 9(c) of Article VII of the NATO SOFA because there was no waiver of confrontation.[39]

(4) The right to have compulsory process for obtaining witnesses in his favor if they are within the jurisdiction of the receiving State (par 9(d), Art. VII, supra)

Although procedural laws of the civil law states provide that an accused may have the court summon witnesses whom he requests, the court has discretion to refuse such requests when it considers that the expected testimony may be irrelevant, cumulative or repetitious.[40] In practice these provisions have been adequate to provide defense witnesses in the cases of United States servicemen who so far have been tried under the Agreement.[41]

One problem of interpretation, however, which might be raised by this safeguard is whether it deprives the court in a civil law country of its discretionary power to refuse to summon a witness for the defense.

The possibility of such a case is illustrated by the following hypothetical situation.

Consider the case of a serviceman tried in Luxembourg who has re-

[38] *Ibid.*

[39] *Ibid.*

[40] See e.g. Federal Republic of Germany, Code of Criminal Prosecution, Art. 259; France, Code de Procédure Pénal (1960), Arts. 281, 323–366, 435, 537; Italy, Procedural Penal Code, Arts. 367, 415; Luxembourg, Code d'Instruction Criminelle, Art. 315; Netherlands, Code of Criminal Procedure, Art. 259; Turkey, Code of Criminal Procedure, Art. 212.

[41] This statement is based on reports of trials on file in the Offices of The Judge Advocates General of the Army, Navy, and Air Force.

quested the Court d'Assises to summon a witness whose testimony he considers to be in his favor. The Cour d'Assises pursuant to Luxembourg law examines the expected testimony of this witness, concludes that the testimony of the witness would be merely cumulative and refuses to summon the witness. The United States trial observer reports that in his opinion the accused has been denied the right to have compulsory process for obtaining witnesses in his favor.

As the testimony of the witness requested by the accused in the hypothetical case is in essence favorable to him, even though cumulative, it would seem that a literal interpretation of paragraph 9(d) requires that the witness be summoned by the court.

On the other hand, it could also be argued that existing practice in civil law states authorizes courts to exercise discretion in the summoning of witnesses and that paragraph 9(d) of Article VII, *supra,* was intended to reflect the existing practice rather than to change it. In this respect an examination of the *travaux préparatoires* does not disclose any intent by the signatories to make such a change in the procedure of civil law countries. Consequently, the accused under paragraph 9(d) of Article VII, *supra,* would have the right to compulsory process for obtaining witnesses who will testify in his favor subject to the court's determination that the expected testimony is material. Under this interpretation, of course, trial proceedings should be closely scrutinized by the United States observer in order to ascertain if there has been any abuse of discretion by the court which would result in a denial of this safeguard.

It would appear that the latter view is the most tenable for the United States to adopt in the hypothetical case. In this respect it should be noted that Article 6 of the United States Constitution which contains the words "to have compulsory process for obtaining witnesses in his favor" has not precluded Federal courts from exercising discretion in the summoning of witnesses.[42]

(5) The right to have legal representation of his own choice for his defense or to have free or assisted legal representation under the conditions prevailing for the time being in the receiving State (par 9(e), Art. VII, supra)

The criminal procedures of all civil law countries which are signatories to the NATO SOF Agreement provide that an accused may have

[42] See *Overholser* v. *DeMarcos,* 149 F. 2d. 23 (1945) CC. A. D. C.) certiorari denied 323 U.S. 889; rehearing denied 326 U.S. 805 where the court denied the request of the

legal representation of his own choice.[43] Further, since the effective date of the NATO SOF Agreement there have been no instances reported where an accused was denied counsel of his choice or was not permitted to have free or assisted legal representation under the conditions prevailing in the receiving state.[44]

In practice, however, United States personnel have rarely utilized the free or assisted legal representation provided by the law of the host states. Rather they understandably have taken advantage of the provisions of title 10, United States Code, section 1037, which provides that the Secretary of each military department and the Department of the Treasury may pay counsel fees, court costs, bail and other expenses incident to the representation *of persons subject to the Uniform Code of Military Justice* before judicial tribunals and any administrative agencies of any foreign nation. In implementing this legislation the Secretaries of the services have authorized payment of counsel fees in both trial and appellate proceedings in cases where the act complained of occurred in the performance of official duty, or where the sentence normally adjudged includes confinement in excess of six months, or where capital punishment might be imposed, or where there is an appeal from any proceeding in which there appears to have been a denial of the substantial rights of the accused or where the case is considered to have significant impact upon the relations of the United States with the host country or involves a particular United States interest.[45] Since the enactment of this law on July 24, 1956 to November 30, 1959 the United States has paid counsel fees in the amount of $168,445.88 in 810 cases involving United States personnel.[46] At the time of the enactment of

accused to obtain the testimony of hospital officials which it determined had nothing to add to the evidence. See also paragraph 137, manual for courts-martial United States, 1951 which provides that a court-martial may limit the number of witnesses called by either side if it appears that the testimony of any excluded witness would be merely cumulative.

[43] See e.g. Belgium, Code d'Instruction Criminelle, Arts. 294, 295; Denmark, Code of Procedure, Secs. 731–732, 823, 925, and 926; Federal Republic of Germany, Code of Criminal Procedure, Sec. 137 (prior to trial, however, the judge may inspect written communications and may attend all oral interviews between the accused and counsel, Sec. 148); France, Code de Procédure Pénale, Arts. 274, 275, 417; Italy, Procedural Penal Code, Arts. 125, 128; Netherlands, Code of Criminal Procedure, Arts. 37–51; Turkey, Code of Criminal Procedure, Art. 136.

[44] This statement is based on the reports of cases filed in the Offices of The Judge Advocates General of the Army, Navy, and Air Force.

[45] See par. 4, Army Regulations 633–55, dated 24 Aug 1956, as changed by changes No. 1, dated 5 May 1958, where this criterion which is typical of the three services is set out. These regulations also set out procedures for the hiring of counsel and payment of expenses and recommends that a judge advocate officer be designated as contracting officer.

[46] See Hearing Before a Subcommittee on Armed Forces, United States Senate on

this legislation members of the civilian component and dependents were considered subject to the Uniform Code of Military Justice in both time of peace and war and enjoyed the benefit of this legislation. Subsequently, however, the Department of Defense determined that such civilian personnel were not entitled to the benefits of title 10, United States Code, section 1037, on the grounds that a recent series of Supreme Court decisions pertaining to the exercise of court-martial jurisdiction over civilians held that such personnel were no longer subject to the Uniform Code of Military Justice in peacetime.[47] The Department of Defense, however, is now sponsoring legislation to amend the provisions of this law to include members of the civilian component and dependents.[48] It may be anticipated that in the interim these categories of United States personnel will take advantage of the law of the receiving state with respect to free or assisted legal representation insofar as they qualify.[49]

(6) The right, if he considers it necessary, to have the services of a competent interpreter (par 9(f), Art. VII, supra)

There have been no problems with respect to the law of any of the receiving states prohibiting the services of an interpreter to an accused. In fact, the criminal procedure of all of the countries which are signato-

Operation of Article VII, NATO Status of Forces Treaty, 85th Cong., 1st sess., April 9, 1957, 8; Hearing of the same subcommittee, 85th Cong., 2d sess., July 29, 1958, 3; Hearing of the same subcommittee, 86th Cong., 1st sess. Aug. 18, 1959, 21.

[47] *Reid* v. *Covert*, 354 U.S. 1 (1957); *Kinsella* v. *Singleton*, 361 U.S. 234 (1960); *Grisham* v. *Hagan*, 361 U.S. 278 (1960); *McElroy* v. *Guagliardo*, 361 U.S. 281 (1960). It is arguable that the administrative action by the Department of Defense to exclude civilian employees and dependents from the purview of 10 U.S.C. 1037 and requesting an amendment of 10 U.S.C. 1037 on the basis of these Supreme Court decisions was premature on the following grounds:

(1) The language "subject to the Uniform Code of Military Justice" as used in 10 U.S.C. 1037 is a short-hand means of reference to identify certain persons entitled to benefits under this legislation at the time it was enacted. Accordingly, the collateral attack on the constitutionality of sections of the Uniform Code of Military Justice with respect to civilians by the recent Supreme Court cases should not impair the efficacy of the words "subject to the Uniform Code of Military Justice" as a descriptive phrase deliminating those persons entitled to benefits under 10 U.S.C. 1037 which is a separate legislative enactment.

(2) The above Supreme Court cases do not preclude the court-martial of members of the civilian component and dependents in wartime and in Berlin where the occupation has not been terminated. Consequently, they are literally still subject to the Uniform Code of Military Justice and thus should continue to be included within the purview of 10 U.S.C. 1037.

[48] Department of Defense Legislative Proposal 87-16 which went to Congress on 3 Jan. 1961.

[49] A representative of The Judge Advocate General of the Army stated that in two cases involving civilians the Department of the Army in this interim period has provided counsel fees from contingency funds of the Secretary of the Army.

ries of the NATO SOF Agreement provide for the services of an interpreter [50] and in practice there has been no denial of this right.[51]

Notwithstanding the fact that receiving states have furnished interpreters there has been some difficulty as to the competency of such personnel. For example, the United States trial observer at the trial of Lt. William E. Roberts, an Air Force officer, in France, reported that the accused was denied the services of a competent interpreter. As a result of this report the military commander who acts for all three services in criminal jurisdiction matters in France investigated the case and ascertained that the interpreter was in fact inadequate, that the President of the Court had recognized this inadequacy and had permitted the United States Air Force interpreter who accompanied the trial observer to assist by translating phrases which the court interpreter could not translate. Because no appeal was taken by the accused and as the accused, who had received a suspended sentence, expressed satisfaction with the ultimate outcome of the case the Department of Defense did not take any further action.[52]

As a result of the Robert's case, however, discussions with the French Ministry of Justice led to permission by the French authorities to utilize interpreters supplied by the United States, where available, for trials and also for audiences before a *juge d'instruction*.[53] A similar practice is followed in Italy and Japan.[54]

As a result of close cooperation between the local United States military authorities and the local foreign authorities in cases requiring interpreters, there have been no cases reported in the last two years in which this right has been denied.[55]

[50] See e.g. Belgium, Code d'Instruction Criminelle, Art. 332; Federal Republic of Germany, Code of Criminal Prosecution, Sec. 259; France, Code de Procédure Pénale, Arts. 102, 272, 344, 407, 535; Italy, Codice de Procedura Penale, Art .326; Luxembourg, Code d'Instruction Criminelle, Art. 332; Netherlands, Code of Criminal Procedure, Arts. 306–308; Norway, Judicature Act of 13 August 1915, Art. 135.

[51] This statement is based on the reports of cases filed in the Offices of The Judge Advocates General of Army, Navy, and Air Force.

[52] For a report of this case see Hearings before a Subcommittee of the Committee on Armed Services on the Operation of Article VII, NATO Status of Forces Treaty, United States Senate, 85th Cong., 2d Sess., July 29, 1958, 41–42.

[53] *Ibid.* See paragraph 4, Section X, French Ministry of Justice Circular 58–16, 4 Sept. 1958, which expressly authorizes French authorities to designate official United States military interpreters as interpreters for French courts because a United States serviceman may use slang or technical expressions which require a knowledge of the English language as spoken in the United States.

[54] The statement is based on the report of cases on file in the Offices of The Judge Advocates General of the Army, Navy, and Air Force. See also Snee and Pye, *Status of Forces Agreement: Criminal Jurisdiction* (1957) 115.

[55] This statement is based on the reports of cases filed in the Offices of The Judge Advocates General of the Army, Navy, and Air Force.

(7) The right to communicate with a representative of the government of the sending States and, when the rules of the court permit, to have such a representative present at his trial (par 9(g), Art. VII, supra)

The right to communicate with a representative of the United States is of the utmost importance to an accused who is confined or otherwise restricted by foreign authorities and subject to judicial and other procedures of a system of law which is totally unfamiliar to him. This right provides an accused with an important defensive measure, namely, the opportunity to receive prompt assistance from the United States to protect his interests.[56] For exemple in certain cases, a United States serviceman under title 10, United States Code, section 1037, would be entitled at the expense of the United States Government to counsel of his choice and the posting of bail. Further, by providing the United States with early notice of his predicament United States authorities would have an opportunity to immediately request the receiving state for a waiver of jurisdiction under paragraph 3(c) of Article VII of the NATO SOFA[57] or to request the release of the serviceman from the custody of the receiving state pending completion of his trial.[58]

Notwithstanding the fact that the provision is silent as to the time at which this right becomes available to the accused, the various receiving states in practice have agreed that United States personnel have the right to promptly communicate with a representative of the United States as soon as they are taken into custody or arrested by the authorities of the receiving state.[59]

The second clause of this provision sets out the right of the accused to have a representative of the United States present at his trial. Although it is a general rule in all of the NATO countries that trials are required to be public, exceptions to this rule are sometimes authorized in cases involving security or sexual offenses.[60]

[56] In respect to notice to the United States par 5(b) of Art. VII, *supra* provides that the authorities of the receiving state are required to promptly notify the military authorities of the United States of the arrest of any member of a force or civilian component or of a dependent of such members.

[57] See note 17, Chapter I.

[58] See par 5, Department of the Army letter, AGAM-P(M) 250.3 (JAGW) 8 April 1958, an executive agency letter, and Sec. IV, E, and "F" Department of Defense Directive 5525.1, May 5, 1962.

[59] This statement is based on the reports of cases on file in the Offices of the Judge Advocates General of the Army, Navy, and Air Force. See also Snee and Pye, *op. cit. supra* note 54, at 114.

[60] Belgium, Constitution, Art, 96; France, Code de Procédural Pénale, Arts. 306, 308, 309, 310; Luxembourg, Constitution, Art. 88; Norway, Criminal Procedural Code, Sec. 112.

In connection with this right consider the hypothetical case of a United States soldier who is tried for an offense against the security of the host state. The judge, as he is permitted to do by the law of the host country, orders that the trial be held *in camera*.[61] The United States trial observer reports that this is a violation of paragraph 9(g) of Article VII of the NATO SOFA on the grounds that, while the public could be excluded, he should not be.

The language of this provision clearly indicates that the United States representative may only be present when the rules of the court permit. An examination of the *travaux préparatoires* of the NATO SOFA discloses that in those cases where the rules of the court do not permit the public to be present it was intended that the representative of the sending state could also be excluded by the judge and that it was for this reason that the words "when the rules of the court permit" were inserted in subparagraph 9(g) of Article VII of the Agreement.[62]

Accordingly, in the hypothetical case the United States would not have a basis for protesting that the exclusion of the United States representative was a denial of this safeguard.[65] It is emphasized, however, that as yet the situation in the hypothetical case has not arisen. In fact, it has been the practice of the authorities of host states with which the United States has agreements to permit the United States trial observers to remain even though the public have been excluded.[64] Although the French Ministry of Justice feels that paragraph 9(g) of Article VII does not compel the admittance of a representative of the sending state to a closed session, it has recommended that such a representative be "among the few persons who are allowed to remain at the hearing."[65] Further, in France United States trial observers

[61] Some examples of countries whose law provide for excluding the public in cases involving security or sexual offenses or those where a minor is involved are Belgium, Constitution, Art. 96; France, Code de Procédure Pénale, Arts. 306, 308, 309, 310, 400; Italy, Codice de Procedura Penal, Art. 423; Luxembourg, Constitution, Art. 88; Netherlands, Code of Criminal Procedure, Art. 273.

[62] Summary Record, MS-D(51)2, Art. 6/7(g); MS-D(51), Art. VII, par. 7(g); MS(J)-R(51)5, pars. 21–25.

[63] In the Japanese Administrative Agreement this problem was avoided by deleting the words "when the rules of the court permit" from this safeguard. See par. 9(g), Art. VII, *T.I.A.S.* 4510.

[64] This statement is based on reports of cases on file in the Offices of The Judge Advocates General of the Army, Navy, and Air Force.

[65] Section VI, French Ministry of Justice Circular 58–16, 4 Sept. 1958, states in pertinent part:

> Sub-paragraph g provides that the accused shall have the right to *communicate* with a representative of the Government of the sending State, and, when the rules of the court permit, to have such a representative present at his trial. The Agreement, having the force of law, authorization to communicate with an accus-

have been admitted even to the preliminary hearings before a *juge d'instruction* which is not a trial and from which the public is generally excluded.[66] It should also be noted that some countries have by internal regulations provided for special notification to the sending state of the trial of a member so that a representative may be present.[67]

ed may not be denied to the appropriate authority, civilian or military, who invokes the benefit of this provision. With respect to the presence of a representative of the Government of the sending State at the trial, it presents a problem only in the case of a trial *in camera*: although the Agreement, which provides the legal rules of procedure, does not in any way make it obligatory, I believe that, should the occasion arise, it would be expedient for the president of the court to admit this representative among the few persons who are permitted to remain in the audience. I consider in a general manner, and I request the magistrates of the Office of Public Prosecution to convey it to the examining magistrates and the presidents, that it is advisable to make an extremely liberal application of this paragraph g. Such cases involve accused persons who run the risk of being surprised by rules of procedure sometimes fundamentally different from those in effect in their countries, who sometimes would be embarrassed thereby in the preparation of their defense, and who, in the very interests of sound justice, must be permitted to surround themselves with all the intellectual and spiritual advice and support appropriate; on return to their country, they might possibly be inclined to find fault with a judicial system which they misunderstand, and it is most desirable to open our courts to better informed and more objective observers: and furthermore, in any case, we have nothing to hide as regards the conditions in which justice is meted out in France.

[66] This information was furnished by a representative of the Office of The Judge Advocate General, Department of the Army, Washington 25, D.C.

[67] Italy, by Article 5 of Decree No. 1666 of December 2, 1956 has provided that:

In the cases contemplated under Article VII, paragraph 9(g) of the Treaty, the President or the Pretore must give timely notice of the date set for the trial to the commanding officer of the unit of which the defendant is a member or, if it not be possible to give such notice or in urgent cases, to the nearest command or office of the sending State, in order that a representative of the Government of said State may be present at the trial.

France by paragraph 2, Section X, Ministry of Justice Circular 58–16, 4 September 1958, has issued similar instructions as follows:

2. The representatives of the American Army in France have received from the Senate of the USA formal instructions to send a *representative who shall attend the trials* every time a person dealt with by the Agreement is prosecuted before a French court of judgment. To permit the practical realization of this help, it is desirable that the Office of Public Prosecution give notice to the American military authorities of the date and the place of hearing, even if a prosecution before the simple police court is involved. The notice shall be addressed to the official who had requested the release, if the latter had been refused, if not, to the superior officers of the accused or, on default, to the nearest official of the same Army; if the case had not given rise to prior correspondence, he shall describe the facts which are the basis for the prosecution.

Normally, this notice shall be transmitted by mail, in case of emergency by telegram or telephone, so as to arrive, except for absolute impossibility, at least three days before the date of the judgment.

One difficulty is liable to arise in the case of prosecutions under the procedures of "flagrante delicto", if the accused does not ask for a term to submit his defense, but accepts an immediate judgment. In anticipation of this eventuality, the

CONCLUSIONS

It may be concluded from the foregoing that the United States has taken adequate safeguards to assure that any denial of a safeguard set out in paragraph 9 of Article VII of the NATO SOFA to a United States seviceman by a court of a receiving state will be promptly reported to the United States authorities. As a result of these measures there is now on file in the Office of The Judge Advocates General of the Army, Navy, and Air Force over 4,000 reports submitted by United States observers of the trials of United States servicemen by the tribunals of NATO countries whose legal systems are different from that of the United States.

An examination of these reports with respect to the application of the procedural safeguards set out in paragraph 9 of Article VII, *supra*, in the trials of United States personnel discloses the following:

(a) The Right to a Prompt and Speedy Trial: In practice there have not been any major problems with this provision. Neither the *travaux préparatoires* of the NATO SOF Agreement nor customary international law set out what constitutes a prompt and speedy trial. In the absence of any definition of a prompt and speedy trial the law of the receiving state as to pretrial and trial procedures must be followed, except that undue delay by the authorities of the receiving state in complying with such procedures might be a denial of the right to a prompt and speedy trial. The United States has successfully protested to the authorities of a receiving state that protracted trial proceedings in cases involving United States servicemen may interfere with the functional operation of the forces of the United States. In consequence, such proceedings have been accelerated.

(b) The Right to be Informed in Advance of Trial of the Specific Charge or Charges Made Against Him: In practice United States servicemen who have been tried by the courts of civil law countries have been provided the advance notice required by this safeguard and there have been no difficulties as to its interpretation.

(c) The Right to be Confronted with the Witnesses Against Him: As a

American authorities in France, who are bound to follow peremptory orders, request that they be notified, by the most rapid means, of the date and the hour of the first appearance before the court in all cases of offenses "flagrante delicto"; they ask, most urgently, that you make it possible for them to send a representative to it, even if they must postpone for several hours, within the legal limits, the moment of this appearance.

Specifically, the notice of the date of hearing must be given to the American authorities, even if a member of a force already repatriated is involved.

result of inherent differences in the common and civil law systems of jurisprudence there is a difference as to the meaning of "confrontation." The United States has accepted the practice of civil law countries that confrontation includes only the right of the accused to be physically present when an adverse witness testified and has not objected that it does not include the common law right of direct cross-examination by the accused. Confrontation of this type may occur before, during, or after the main trial. Further, the United States has not protested *in absentia* trials in civil law countries when the accused consents to be so tried on the theory that the accused has waived his right to confrontation, but would undoubtedly protest such trials in those cases where he has not waived his right to confrontation.

(d) The Right to Have Compulsory Process for Obtaining Witnesses in his Favor if They are Within the Jurisdiction of the Receiving State: This provision should not be interpreted as depriving the court in a civil law country of its discretion to refuse to summon a witness for the defense on the grounds that the expected testimony of the witness may be irrelevant, cumulative or repetitious. Rather, it should be interpreted as providing the accused with the right to compulsory process for obtaining witnesses who will testify in his favor subject to the court's discretion. Trial proceedings, however, should be closely scrutinized to determine if there has been any abuse of discretion by the court which would result in a denial of this safeguard. In practice the procedures of civil law countries have been adequate to provide defense witnesses to United States servicemen tried under the agreement.

(e) The Right to have Legal Representation of his Own Choice for his Defense or to have Free or Assisted Legal Representation Under the Conditions Prevailing for the Time Being in the Receiving State: The criminal procedures of all civil law countries who are signatories of the NATO SOFA provide that an accused may have legal representation of his own choice and there have not been any instances where an accused was denied counsel of his choice or was not permitted to have free or assisted legal representation under the conditions prevailing in the receiving state. In practice, United States servicemen rarely utilize the free or assisted legal representation provided by the law of the host state. Rather, they prefer to take advantage of United States legislation which authorizes the payment of counsel fees, court costs, bail, and other expenses by the United States.

(f) The Right, if he Considers it Necessary, to have the Services of a Competent Interpreter: The criminal procedure of all of the countries

which are signatories of the NATO SOFA provide for the services of an interpreter and in practice there has been no denial of this right. Some difficulty, however, has been experienced with respect to competency of interpreters furnished by receiving states. These difficulties have been corrected and as a result of close cooperation between the local United States military authorities and the local foreign authorities there have been no cases reported in the past two years in which this right was denied.

(g) The Right to Communicate with a Representative of the Government of the Sending State and, When the Rules of the Court Permit, to have such a Representative Present at his Trial: In practice there has been no denial by any of the signatories of the NATO SOFA of the right of the accused to communicate with a representative of his state and as a rule United States servicemen have been permitted to promptly communicate with a representative of the United States as soon as they are taken into custody or arrested by the authorities of the receiving state. Although there have not been any cases where a representative of the United States has been excluded from the trial of a United States serviceman there would probably be no basis for the United States to protest such an exclusion if it were consistent with the rules of the court.

In summary it may be concluded that in the more than 4,000 cases of United States personnel tried by the tribunals of civil law countries during the past eight years there have been no major differences between the United States and such countries as to the application and interpretation of the safeguards set out in paragraph 9 of Article VII of the NATO SOF Agreement with the exception of paragraph 9(d) which pertains to confrontation. Further, during this period in only one of these cases, the *Baldwin* case [68] has there been diplomatic intervention by the United States because of a denial of a safeguard under the procedure set forth in paragraph 4 of the Senate Resolution.[69]

The favorable experience in the implementation of the NATO "fair trial" safeguards enjoyed by the United States and those NATO nations whose systems of law are different in whole or in part from that of the United States has been largely the result of their accommodation of each other's interests.

Some instances of this accommodation on the part of the authorities of NATO countries are their accelerating the trials of United States servicemen, their permitting a serviceman to promptly communicate

[68] See Hearings, *op. cit. supra* note 30.
[69] See Appendix 1.

with a representative of the United States upon his arrest, and their admitting a United States observer to sessions of a trial of a United States serviceman from which the public are excluded. Adjunctively, the military authorities of the United States have viewed foreign legal systems different from their own with sympathy and understanding and have cooperated with foreign authorities in the administration of justice in cases involving United States personnel.

The absence of any major controversy between the United States and these NATO countries illustrates how nations having different legal systems and cultures may, through an informal "backdoor" approach, interact with and upon each other in a social process to shape desirable community prescriptions which will promote a common goal. The common goal in this instance is the advancement of national self-defense by interdependence with other nations. Without this mutuality of interest, it is probable that overemphasis by the participating countries on technical rules and legal norms in the implementation of the NATO "fair trial" safeguards might have reaped dissension and contumely.

CHAPTER IV

DENIAL OF 'FAIR TRIAL' SAFEGUARDS AND UNITED STATES FORCES

The purpose of this chapter is to consider what redress a United States serviceman may have under international law and United States domestic law if he is denied a "fair trial" safeguard by a NATO country. Its theme is best illustrated by considering the hypothetical case of a United States serviceman who is tried by the courts of a NATO country and during the trial is denied summarily the right to have compulsory process to obtain witnesses in his favor as provided by paragraph 9(d) of Article VII of the NATO SOF Agreement. The serviceman is convicted and sentenced to a fine. Under international law[1] what action may be taken by the serviceman or the United States because of denial of this safeguard by the host state?

(a) By the Serviceman

It is a well-established rule of international law that, absent an international agreement by states, an individual, such as the serviceman in the hypothetical case, does not possess an international personality.[2] States, however, by a *pactum in favores tertii* may accord individuals rights, duties, and responsibilities, including a capacity for procedural action.[3] The international personality so accorded the individual is

[1] The present inquiry does not consider the remedy a United States serviceman may have under the municipal law of the receiving state. In this respect it should be noted that the constitutions of some states provide that treaties are part of the municipal law. For example, Art. 55 of the new French Constitution (Oct. 4, 1958) provides: "Treaties or agreements duly ratified or approved shall, upon their publication, have an authority superior to that of laws..."

[2] See 1 Oppenheim, *International Law* (8th ed., Lauterpacht 1955) 20 where it is stated that "also, although States are the normal subjects of International Law they may treat individuals and other persons as endowed directly with international rights and duties and constitute them to that extent subjects of International Law" and Briggs, *The Law of Nations, Cases, Documents and Notes* 95 (1952). See also Korowicz, *Introduction to International Law*, 324 ff. (1959) for a comprehensive discussion of the individual as a subject of international law.

[3] Some instances where states have by international agreement accorded individuals

dependent on the will of states and is always revocable by them.

Accordingly, the action the serviceman in the hypothetical case may take under international law because of the denial of the safeguard set out in paragraph 9(d), Article VII of the NATO SOFA will depend upon the degree of legal personality accorded him in that agreement by the states concerned. It is thus necessary to determine whether the NATO SOFA accords the serviceman a personal right to the safeguards set out in paragraph 9 of Article VII, *supra,* and a capacity to protect such right.

An examination of paragraph 9 of Article VII of the NATO SOFA[4] discloses that the language delimiting these safeguards is personal in nature. It contains such words and phrases as "he shall be entitled," "made against him," "witnesses in his favor," "legal representation of his own choice for his defense," "if he considers it necessary," and "present at his trial." This language clearly demonstrates that the signatories of the Agreement have coupled these safeguards to the individual and to this extent the serviceman in the hypothetical case has acquired under international law a personal right to these safeguards. In corroboration of this view, the United States in practice has taken the position that an accused United States serviceman may waive any of the safeguards set out in paragraph 9 of Article VII, *supra,* by refusing to appeal his case to a higher tribunal of the receiving state. In such instances the United States has not protested the denial of a safeguard provided by paragraph 9 of Article VII, *supra,* by the lower tribunal of the receiving state.[5]

a limited international personality are as follows: (1) The Central American Court of Justice which was created by the Treaty of Washington of December 20, 1907, and before which individuals of one of the five signatories were permitted to assert claims directly against one of the other four signatories according to Article 2, paragraphs b and c of the Treaty; (2) The German-Polish Upper Silesia Convention of May 15, 1922, under which individuals were granted the capacity directly to claim their vested rights before an international tribunal not only against a foreign government but also against their own government; (3) The Convention on the Political Rights of Women of December 20, 1952, which creates or guarantees important substantive rights for individuals, but does not provide for a capacity for international legal action of these individuals in order to protect by themselves their rights under international law; (4) private individuals and corporations have the right to legal action before the Court of Justice of the European Coal and Steel Community which was constituted in December 1952 by six states on the basis of an international agreement; and (5) The European Convention for the Protection of Human Rights and Fundamental Freedoms of November 4, 1950, which guarantees individuals certain substantive human rights and which by Article 25 provides individuals certain limited access to the European Commission of Human Rights.

[4] See Appendix 3.

[5] See Hearings Before a Subcommittee of the Committee on Armed Services, on the Operation of Article VII, NATO Status of Forces Treaty, United States Senate, 84th

In view of the above it appears that the serviceman in the hypothetical case has been accorded a personal right to the safeguards set out in paragraph 9 of Article VII, *supra*, and to that extent at least he possesses an international personality.

A further examination of the NATO SOFA, however, discloses that it does not provide the serviceman in the hypothethetical case with the procedural capacity under international law to enforce his right by himself. Further, in the present practice of international law there does not exist any international judicial body or other tribunal before which the serviceman could attempt to enforce the procedural safeguards set out in paragraph 9 of Article VII, *supra*.[6]

In view of the above it is concluded that although the serviceman in the hypothetical case possesses an international personality to the extent of having been accorded a right to the safeguards set out in paragraph 9 of Article VII, *supra*, he does not possess the procedural capacity under international law to enforce this right by himself directly against the host country. Consequently, under international law he is not able take any action in the hypothetical case because of the denial by the host state of his right to have compulsory process to obtain witnesses in his favor as provided by paragraph 9(d) of Article VII, *supra*.

(b) By the United States

As the serviceman in the hypothetical case lacks the capacity under international law to protect his rights to the procedural safeguard which the host country has denied him, he must rely for this protection upon the United States. Under the law of nations states are the principal subjects of international law[7] and as a state the United States under a well recognized rule of customary international law has a right to protest through diplomatic channels to another state which has wrongfully injured its national abroad.[8] In this respect the World Court has stated

Cong., 1st Sess., March 29, 31 and June 21, 1955, 59 and the same Hearings, United States Senate, 85th Cong., 2d Sess., July 29, 1958, 42.

[6] In Lauterpacht, *International Law and Human Rights*, 27, 54 (1950) it is stated that a right may exist even though there is no power on the part of the individual to assert it. In this respect it is interesting to note that the World Court in the *Peter Pazmany University Case*, Series A/B, No. 61, 231, stated: "It is scarcely necessary to point out that the capacity to possess civil rights does not necessarily imply the capacity to exercise these rights oneself." See also Korowicz, *op. cit. supra* note 2, at 345 who characterizes individuals who have rights without the capacity to enforce them under international law before international bodies as "only passive subjects of international law."

[7] 1 Oppenheim, *op. cit. supra* note 2, at 19.

[8] 1 Oppenheim, *op. cit. supra* note 2, at 686.

that the home state of an injured alien does not merely substitute itself for the alien but rather asserts its own right to insure in the person of its subjects, respect for the rules of international law.[9] Further, as there is no rule of international law which imposes a duty upon the home state of the alien to initiate such a diplomatic protest, the United States, unless its domestic law requires otherwise, has discretion as to whether or not it will pursue this course of action.[10]

In the hypothetical case, this rule of customary international law is reflected in the provisions of Article XVI[11] of the NATO SOFA which requires that any differences between the contracting parties relating to the interpretation or application of the Agreement shall be settled by negotiation between them without recourse to any outside jurisdiction. It further provides that, except where express provision is made to the contrary in the Agreement, differences which cannot be settled by negotiation shall be referred to the North Atlantic Council.[12] The *travaux préparatoires* disclose that these provisions would preclude the reference of a dispute to the World Court unless all the parties agreed to do so.[13]

Under Article XVI the United States in the hypothetical case may insist through diplomatic channels that the host state take appropriate action to correct the failure of the local court to accord the United States serviceman the procedural safeguards set out in paragraph 9(d) of Article VII of the Agreement. The theoretical basis of the United States action would be that the host country has apparently breached a provision of an international agreement between the United States and the host state by its denial to the United States serviceman of a procedural safeguard accorded to him paragraph 9 of the Agreement.

It should be noted that under Article XVI of the NATO SOF Agreement the United States is entitled to intervene diplomatically in the

[9] "Mavrommatis Palestine Concession Case," *P.C.I.J.* (1924) Series A, No. 2, p. 12.

[10] 1 Oppenheim, *op. cit. supra* note 2, at 686–7; Jessup, *A Modern Law of Nations*, 98 (1952).

[11] Art. XVI provides: "All differences between the Contracting Parties relating to the interpretation or application of this Agreement shall be settled by negotiation between them without recourse to any outside jurisdiction. Except where express provision is made to the contrary in this Agreement, differences which cannot be settled by direct negotiation shall be referred to the North Atlantic Council."

[12] A representative of the Department of State has advised that to date there have been no disputes under Article VII referred to the North Atlantic Council.

[13] With respect to the provision prohibiting "recourse to any outside jurisdiction," the *Summary Record*, Doc. MS(J)-R(51) 9, pars 21, 22 discloses that the French representative asked the Working Group whether Art. XVI prevented the reference of a dispute to the International Court of Justice at The Hague. The chairman stated that this was so unless all parties agreed to do so.

hypothetical case even though the denial of the safeguard by the host country has taken place at the trial court level. The so-called "exhaustion of local remedies" rule[14] is applicable only when a state puts forward an international claim on behalf of an alien on account of an alleged denial of justice. Such a claim will not be entertained unless the alien has been unable to obtain redress through the local remedies provided by the host state.[15]

It is now proposed to amplify the hypothetical situation previously set out as follows:

> The United States military authorities report the denial of the safeguard to the Department of State and request that the Secretary of State through diplomatic channels insist that the host state take appropriate action to correct the failure of the trial court to accord the serviceman the procedural safeguards set out in paragraph 9(d) of Article VII, *supra*. The Secretary of State refuses to comply with this request on the grounds that as only a fine was adjudged against the serviceman the case was not serious enough to run the risk of jeopardizing the relations of the United States with the host state. These relations are already at a low level and the Department of State feels that the host state would probably construe a diplomatic protest on the part of the United States as an unwarranted interference in its internal affairs. The United States serviceman in the hypothetical case then petitions the United States District Court for the District of Columbia for a mandatory order compelling the Secretary of State to intervene with the host State to protect his right to the safeguard set out in paragraph 9(d) of Article VII of the NATO SOFA. In support of his petition the serviceman argues: that the provisions of paragraph 9 of Article VII of the NATO SOFA accord him a right to the safeguards set out therein; that the United States by ratifying the NATO SOFA has joined with the other signatories of the Agreement in according him this right; that as the NATO SOFA is a Treaty made under the authority of the United States it is part of the law of the land[16] and the United States courts are bound to enforce the rights it accords to him; that it was the intent of the Senate in paragraph 4 of its

[14] 1 Oppenheim, *op. cit. supra* note 2, at 361; Schwarzenberger, International Law, Vol 1, *International Law as Applied by International Courts and Tribunals:* 1 (3d ed. 1957) 606.

[15] See "Interhandel Case," *I.C.J. Reports* (1959) p. 27 (21 March 1959) which reiterates this rule.

[16] Article VI, Clause 2, Constitution.

resolution of advice and consent to the ratification of the NATO SOF Agreement [17] that the Department of State would take appropriate action to protect the rights of the accused in the event there was a denial of one of the safeguards set out in paragraph 9 of Article VII of the Agreement; that there is no doubt that the host state has denied the serviceman the right set out in paragraph 9(d) of Article VII and that this denial is admitted by the Department of State; that the mandatory order which is sought is therefore for the performance of a duty required by law; and that if the request is denied the serviceman will have a right without a remedy as he has no procedural capacity under international law to protect his right.

Under United States domestic law what would be the probable result of this action by the United States serviceman?

The hypothetical situation as amplified presents the provocative question of whether under United States domestic law the Judicial Branch may compel the Executive Branch to intervene with the host state in order to protect the right accorded the United States serviceman under paragraph 9(d), Article VII of the NATO SOF Agreement. An inquiry into the Federal Constitution, interpretive decisions of the Supreme Court, and the NATO SOF Agreement is necessary to resolve this question.

The writ of mandamus was known to the common law and it is of ancient origin. It is said to have been devised to prevent disorder from a failure of justice and was used to compel the performance of a specific duty in cases where the ordinary forms of legal procedure did not furnish an adequate remedy.[18]

An examination of United States Supreme Court decisions discloses that the subordinates through whom the President acts may be compelled by mandamus to perform their ministerial duties.[19] In this respect it has been held that a duty is ministerial when the law prescribes and defines the duty to be performed with such precision and certainty as to leave nothing to the exercise of discretion and judgment.[20] Some examples of acts by various executive officers which have been charac-

[17] See Appendix 1 (Senate Resolution).

[18] 55 *C.J.S.* 2.

[19] *Kendall* v. *U.S.*, 12 Pet. 524 (1938); *United States* v. *Schurz*, 102 U.S. 378 (1880); *U.S. Ex rel Dunlap* v. *Block*, 128 U.S. 40 (1888). Cf. *Decatur* v. *Paulding*, 14 Pet. 497 (1840); and *Riverside Oil Co.* v. *Hitchcock*, 190 U.S. 316 (1903), where the rule is reiterated that mandamus will not lie against an officer to control him in the exercise of an official duty which requires the exercise of his judgment and discretion.

[20] *Wilbur* v. *U.S. ex rel Kadrie*, 281 U.S. 206 (1930); *Kendall* v. *U.S.*, *supra*.

terized as ministerial are the crediting by the Postmaster-General of an award by the Solicitor to the Treasury, [21] the delivery of a commission to which the petitioner is entitled by law,[22] the payment of a warrant by the Secretary of the Treasury under a statute, [23] the delivery of a patent for certain public lands which had been regularly signed, sealed, countersigned, and duly recorded,[24] and the payment by the Secretary of State of money to which petitioner has a right by law.[25]

On the other hand, the writ of mandamus will not lie in a case where its effect is to direct or control executive officers in the discharge of an executive duty requiring the exercise of judgment or discretion.[26] It has been stated as a rule that "In matters which require judgment and consideration to be exercised by an executive officer of the government or which are dependent upon his discretion, no rule for a mandamus to control his action will issue. It is only for ministerial acts of which no exercise of discretion is required, that the rule will be granted."[27]

From the principles set out above it appears that a writ of mandamus would lie against the Secretary of State in the hypothetical situation if the duty requested of him by the serviceman is ministerial and the obligation to intervene with the host state is required by law in a clear and indisputable manner. Accordingly, in order to determine if the mandamus would lie in the hypothetical situation it is necessary to ascertain whether the nature of the act to which the writ is directed is ministerial.

It is well established that the President plays a dominant role in the determination of the foreign policy of the United States and that he enjoys a wide discretion in the exercise of this power.[28] In this respect it has been authoritatively stated that the President is the only organ of communication of the United States with foreign governments and that

[21] *Kendall* v. *U.S.*, *supra*.

[22] *Marbury* v. *Madison*, 1 Cr. 137 (1803).

[23] *U.S.* v. *MacVeagh*, 214 U.S. 124 (1909).

[24] *U.S.* v. *Schurz*, *supra*.

[25] *U.S.* v. *Bayard*, 16 D.C. 428 (1887), 5 *Machey's Rpts* 428.

[26] *Decatur* v. *Paulding*, *supra; U.S. ex rel International Contracting Company* v. *Lamont*, 155 U.S. 303, 308 (1894); *U.S. ex rel Riverside Oil Co.* v. *Hitchcock supra; Ness* v. *Fisher*, 223 U.S. 683 (1912); *Roughton* v. *Ickes*, 101 F. 2d 248 (1938).

[27] *U.S. ex rel Carrick* v. *Lamar*, 116 U.S. 423 (1886); *Hammond* v. *Hull*, 76 App. D.C. 301, 131 F. 2d 23 (1942); *Yee Giving Mee* v. *Acherm*, D.C. N.D. Cal. S.D. 108 F. Supp. 502 (1952).

[28] See Garner, "Executive Discretion in the Conduct of Foreign Relations," 31 *A.J. I.L.* 289 (1937); Corwin, *The President's Control of Foreign Relations* (1922); Berdahl, *The War Powers of the Executive in the U.S.* (1920) and the speech of Senator Spooner n the Senate in 1906 (56th *Cong. Record*, 1st Sess., Vol XL, Pt. 2, p. 1417 ff.)

he may shape the foreign policies of the United States.[29] The Executive thus has discretion to determine when, how, and upon what subjects negotiations with foreign countries may be urged with the greatest prospect of success.[30] It is therefore apparent that the initiation of diplomatic negotiations by the Executive requires the exercise of judgment and discretion. Consequently, it may be stated as a general rule that the initiation of such negotiations is not a ministerial act imposed upon the Executive by law.

Do the facts and circumstances set out in the hypothetical case warrant any departure from this general rule?

The substance of the argument of petitioner is that he has been granted a right by paragraph 9 of Article VII of the NATO SOF Agreement which, as a treaty of the United States is part of the law of the land and that under international law only the Executive can intervene with the host state to protect this right. He maintains that if he cannot compel the Secretary of State to intervene he has a right without a remedy.

By virtue of the NATO SOFA the United States has joined with the other signatories in granting the serviceman a personal right under international law. Further, under United States domestic law the United States would be bound to accord the rights set forth in paragraph 9 of Article VII, *supra*, to a foreign serviceman tried in a United States Court.[31] In the hypothetical case, however, the only assistance it can render the United States serviceman is to intervene diplomatically with the host country. Normally, the initiation of such negotiations is a matter solely within the discretion of the Executive. There is no United States statute which directs that the Executive must intervene in cases where a host country has denied a United States serviceman a right set out in paragraph 9 of Article VII, *supra*.[32] In fact, it appears

[29] Corwin, *The President*, 225 (1957); Byrd, *Treaties and Executive Agreements in the U.S.* 177 (1960); Pomeroy, *Constitutional Law*, 564 (1888). See the statement of John Marshal which was made in the House of Representatives on March 7, 1800 that "the President is the sole organ of the nation in its external relations, and its sole representative with foreign nations." (*Annals*, 6th Cong., Vol 613) and the opinion of Justice Sutherland in *U.S.* v. *Curtiss-Wright Export Corporation*, 299 U.S. 304 (1936) wherein he concludes that based on the inherent power of the federal government to control foreign affairs, only the President can speak or listen in such field as a representative of the nation.

[30] See *U.S.* v. *Curtiss-Wright*, *supra* note 29, at 319 where Mr. Justice Sutherland quoted this statement from a report of the Senate Committee on Foreign Relations (Feb. 15, 1816) with approval.

[31] See Ellert, "The United States as a Receiving State," 63 *Dickinson L.R.* 75 (1959); Cf. *Ware* v. *Hylton*, 3 Dall. 199 (1796); *Head Money Cases*, 112 U.S. 589, 598 (1884).

[32] The constitutionality of such legislation may be doubtful as it appears to be a

that the United States Senate expressly recognized that the duty to intervene was not mandatory when it stated in its resolution of advice and consent to the ratification of the NATO SOF Agreement that the military authorities should request the Department of State to take "appropriate action to protect the rights of the accused."[33] The word "appropriate" is in this context a word of discretion. It connotes the sense of the Senate that the Executive will decide what action, if any, will be taken. Thus, the Senate Resolution may not be interpreted as a fiat which imposes a duty upon the Secretary of State to undertake diplomatic negotiations in all cases where there has been a denial of the rights set forth in paragraph 9 of Article VII, *supra*. Further, it does not appear that the 5th Amendment of the Constitution which states pertinently that no person shall "be deprived of life, liberty, or property, without due process of law" imposes a duty upon the Executive to intervene. Clearly, this amendment refers only to deprivation of life, liberty, or property which is by an act of the Federal Government.[34] It is thus inapplicable to the hypothetical situation where it is an act of a foreign government which deprives the United States serviceman of his property. Accordingly, the facts and circumstances of the hypothetical situation do not appear to alter the general rule that the initiation of diplomatic negotiations with a foreign government is discretionary and not a ministerial act.

In the recent case of *Keefe v. Dulles*,[35] which also involved the NATO SOFA and the Senate Resolution thereto, a lower Federal court similarly came to the conclusion that the initiation of diplomatic negotiations with a foreign government is a discretionary duty on the part of the Executive.

In this case two United States soldiers stationed in France were tried in a French court under the criminal jurisdictional formula set out in paragraph 3 of Article VII of the NATO SOFA. They pleaded guilty and were sentenced to confinement in a French prison. The United States observer who was present at the trial reported that there was no violation of the safeguards provided by paragraph 9 of Article VII of the NATO SOF Agreement. The relatrix, the wife of one of the soldiers, filed a petition which alleged, *inter alia*, that the Secretary of State

usurpation by the legislative body of an inherent duty of the Executive Branch to conduct foreign affairs. See *U.S.* v. *Curtiss-Wright, supra*.

[33] See Appendix 1.

[34] *Barron use of Tierman* v. *Baltimore*, 7 Pet. 243 (1833).

[35] 222 *Fed. Reporter*, 2d, 390 (1954) Writ of Certiorari denied, Feb. 28, 1955, 75 S. Ct. 440.

could by representation to the Government of France obtain the release of relatrix's husband. The District Court granted respondent's motion to discharge a show cause order and dismissed the petition. Relatrix appealed. On appeal the court deemed the petition sufficient as one seeking a mandatory order requiring the Secretary of State to obtain Keefe's release through diplomatic negotiations with France. The court considered the provision of the reservation of the United States Senate at the time it gave its consent and advice to the ratification of the NATO SOF Agreement which stated that a United States observer shall attend the trial of each United States serviceman and report to his commanding officer any violation of the safeguards set out in paragraph 9 of Article VII of the NATO SOF Agreement, whereupon in the event of such a violation that officer "shall then request the Department of State to take appropriate action to protect the rights of the accused." It pointed out, however, that no such violation had been reported and the State Department had not been requested by the military authorities to take action. The court then stated, "Even had the request been made, whether to grant it would have been within the Secretary's discretion. He was not under a legal duty to attempt through diplomatic processes to obtain Keefe's release. Quite to the contrary, the commencement of diplomatic negotiations with a foreign power is completely in the discretion of the President and the head of the Department of State, who is his political agent. The Executive is not subject to judicial control or direction in such matters. Accordingly, we hold the petition was properly dismissed, even though it be regarded as seeking affirmative injunctive relief against the Secretary of State."[36] In this rationale, the court relied on *Marbury* v. *Madison*[37] and *United States* v. *Curtiss-Wright Export Corp.*[38]

SUMMARY

It is concluded from the foregoing that although the signatories of the NATO SOF Agreement have accorded the United States serviceman in the hypothetical case a right to the safeguards set out in paragraph 9 of Article VII of that Agreement, the serviceman has not been provided any procedural capacity under international law by which he himself may protect his right. In the event of a denial of a procedural

[36] *Id.* at 393–394.
[37] *Supra*, note 22.
[38] *Supra*, note 29.

safeguard provided by the NATO SOF Agreement a United States serviceman under international law must rely on the United States to intervene with the host state to protect his right. Further, under United States domestic law, if the Secretary of State refuses to so intervene, the Federal courts would probably not compel such intervention as negotiation with a foreign state is not a ministerial duty.[39] Accordingly, from the viewpoint of the serviceman in the hypothetical case the right accorded him by paragraph 9d of the NATO SOF Agreement is somewhat meaningless as he lacks the capacity to enforce it himself. Consequently, it may be stated that he possesses at most a passive or inchoate right to the safeguards set out in paragraph 9 of Article VII, *supra*.

[39] May Congress compel such intervention? See 22 *U.S.C.* 1732 which directs the President to intervene and demand the release of a United States citizen wrongfully imprisoned by a foreign government.

CHAPTER V

MINIMUM STANDARD OF PROCEDURAL JUSTICE

In Chapter III it was concluded that during the past eight years the NATO "fair trial" safeguards have been successfully implemented in thousands of cases among countries having different legal systems and different cultures. This success was largely the result of an informal reciprocal decision making process in which the participants shared the goal of mutual defense.

The purpose of this chapter is to demonstrate how the experience of these NATO countries in the implementation of the NATO "fair trial" safeguards among different systems of law may be utilized to achieve a minimum standard of procedural justice for all aliens and, ultimately, for all persons.

Under traditional international law, an alien, as an individual, does not possess an international personality.[1] The consequence of this lack of status of the alien is that if he is injured by a host state and unable to obtain satisfaction in the ordinary domestic channels provided by the offending state he has no avenue by which he may personally secure redress under international law.[2] To ameliorate this condition there developed a rule of customary international law that a host state may become responsible to the home state of the alien, if not to the alien, for any injury or damage to the alien which is caused by an act or omission of the host state that is contrary to or wrongful under international law.[3] This rule was based on the Vattelian fiction of the injury to the state through the injury of its national.[4]

There was never established, however, any customary rule of international law which prescribed the minimum procedural safeguards which a host state must accord an alien who is prosecuted in its courts,

[1] Chapter IV, at 45.
[2] *Id.* at 47.
[3] Chapter II, at 9.
[4] *Id.* at 8.

the denial of which would be contrary to or wrongful under international law.[5]

The failure of such a customary rule of international law to develop was primarily due to a disagreement among two groups of states as to the standard to be used in measuring the minimum procedural safeguards which a host state must accord in the prosecution of an alien.[6]

One group of states urged that customary international law only required them to provide in the prosecution of an alien those safeguards which they accorded to their own nationals.[7] Under this theory, commonly called the "national treatment" theory, a denial of a procedural safeguard in the prosecution of an alien would be contrary to or wrongful under international law only if the national of the host state would be entitled under its domestic law to such a safeguard.

On the other hand, an equally substantial group of states asserted that there is a customary rule of international law which provided that there is a minimum standard of procedural justice according to which all aliens are entitled to be treated.[8] Under this theory any denial by the host state in the prosecution of an alien of a procedural safeguard prescribed by this standard would be considered contrary to or wrongful under international law. In such a case the host country would not be entitled to the defense that its nationals were similarly treated. Conversely, a "minimum standard" state would not admit that an alien was entitled to more than the procedural safeguards set out in the minimum standard simply because its own nationals were so treated under its domestic law.

Neither of the two groups of states questioned the customary rule of international law pertaining to state responsibility in the abstract, i.e., that a host state may become responsible to the home state of an alien for any injury or damage to the alien which is caused by an act or omission which is contrary to or wrongful under international law. Their controversy concerned the criteria to be applied in determining the minimum procedural safeguards to which an alien was entitled. The practical effect of this lack of agreement was to establish two different criteria for ascertaining the procedural safeguards to which an alien was entitled if prosecuted by a host state. Both the "national treatment" states and the "minimum standard" states, however, would recognize a claim of the home state of an alien for injury or damage to

[5] *Id.* at 20.
[6] *Id.* at 19.
[7] *Id.* at 13.
[8] *Id.* at 16.

the alien if it were caused by a denial of a procedural safeguard contained in their respective criteria.

The following hypothetical case illustrates the handicaps traditional international law imposes upon an alien who may have been denied a procedural safeguard in a prosecution by the host state.

An alien engaged in commercial activities in a host country assaults a local policeman who attempts to arrest him for being drunk and disorderly. The alien is tried and convicted for this offense and sentenced to imprisonment for one year. During the trial the alien was denied the services of an interpreter even though he does not speak or understand the local language. The alien feels his conviction is unjust as he had no opportunity to prepare a defense against the evidence introduced against him. His subsequent appeal to the highest court of the host country is denied.

Under traditional international law the alien in the hypothetical case would have no way of personally securing redress in the international arena against the host state as he does not possess an international personality. Under traditional international law he would have to rely on his home state to press a claim in its own behalf for any damages he may have suffered by being denied an interpreter. The home state, however, in complete disregard of the desires of the alien could agree in its negotiations with the host state to drop, compromise or otherwise dispose of the claim. Further, in view of the dichotomy between the "national treatment" states and the "minimum standard" states the home state under existing international law could not even establish that there is any customary rule of international law which prescribes that an interpreter must be accorded in the prosecution of an alien who does not speak or understand the local language. Accordingly, traditional international law provides the alien with no effective means of obtaining redress for the denial of an interpreter by the host state. He must rely on his home state to press his claim and, even then, there is no rule of international law which the home state may cite as requiring the host state to furnish an interpreter. It is proposed to suggest in this chapter a solution which would ameliorate the unfavorable situation of the alien in the hypothetical case.

In view of the dichotomy among nations as to whether the "national treatment" or "minimum standard" theory should be used to determine the minimum procedural safeguards which a host state has a duty to accord an alien prosecuted in its courts, there is serious doubt that either theory will ever be accepted as a rule of international law. Further, even if one or the other of these theories were accepted as a rule of international law it is questionable whether either of them provides criteria which would assure uniform safeguards in the trials of aliens by different countries throughout the world. The "national treatment" theory by its nature will vary from state to state and the "minimum standard" theory lacks precision and is a hopeless failure as a definitive norm.[9]

If aliens prosecuted in a court of a host state are to be accorded uniform minimum procedural safeguards, a basis other than the "national treatment" theory or the "minimum standard" theory is needed.

In arriving at such a basis the main objection of the nations favoring the "national treatment" theory to the "minimum standard" theory must be considered. These states being new and relatively weak feared that the "minimum standard" theory was so vague as to permit unbridled interference by stronger powers in their internal affairs. They believed that under the "minimum standard" theory almost any departure from the procedural safeguards of the home country of the alien could be alleged by that country as being contrary to or wrongful under international law. In consequence the world decision making process failed to achieve uniformity as to the minimum procedural safeguards to be accorded aliens because of the lack of a basis mutally acceptable to all nations.

Accordingly, it would appear that the minimum procedural safeguards for aliens contained in any new basis must be specific as to content and acceptable to all major legal systems in order to allay any suspicion on the part of weaker nations that they would be a vehicle for unlimited interference with their internal affairs. Once such a mutual basis is formulated, an appropriate vehicle to obtain its acceptance by states would be a universal multilateral convention.[10] This procedure would nullify the current controversy between the "national treatment" theory and the "minimum standard" theory as to the minimum procedural safeguards to be accorded an alien by a host country. Among those states parties to such a multilateral convention there would be uniform criteria for establishing the minimum procedural safeguards to which an alien would be entitled.

In setting out these criteria in a multilateral convention should they

[9] *Id.* at 16, 19.

[10] Such as that being undertaken by the International Law Commission on state responsibility at the request of the General Assembly. See Resolution 799 (VIII) of the General Assembly, 7 Dec 1959.

be drafted as rights of the alien's home state or as direct rights of the alien?

It would be consistent with traditional international law if they are set out as rights of the alien's home state.[11] Under such a formulation the host state would be responsible solely to the home state for a denial of a safeguard to the alien. This rule at best was designed to protect the alien within the existing framework of international law. To do this states indulged in the fiction of the injury to the state through the injury to its national. How valid is it to continue this pretense? The home state may refuse to intervene with the host state, may intervene against the will of the alien, may accept a compromise settlement with the host state or may even waive the wrong done to its national altogether. The injury to the alien thus becomes entwined with the relations between the home state of the alien and the host state and appropriate satisfaction to the alien may be contingent on these relations. Dunn pointed this out when he stated that the denial of international status to the individual has caused the activities of men as human beings to be subordinated to the political relations of states.[12] Brierly believes that the jettisoning of this old fiction and the recognition that it is the individual who is injured would promote world peace as claims of states for injuries to individuals would not become coupled to "that mysterious but potent abstraction, "national honor" and could also serve to preclude states from promoting claims of aliens which economically they identify with their national interest.[13] Jessup, additionally, brings out that under existing law in some situations, such as disputes over administration of mandated areas, the state must not only espouse a claim but also make it the subject of an insoluble diplomatic controversy before the matter can be submitted to an international tribunal.[14] Further, certain illogical rules have developed concerning the nationality of claims as a consequence of the fact that under traditional international law a state may not make diplomatic representations to another state on behalf of an individual who is not its national. Thus, a stateless person under traditional international law is completely excluded from having a claim presented in his behalf because he, as an individual, has no status under traditional international law and an injury to him by

[11] See Chapter II.

[12] Dunn, "The International Rights of Individuals," 1941 *Am. Soc. Int. L. Proc.* 14, 16, 17.

[13] Brierly, "Le Fondement de Caractère obligatoire du droit international," 23 *Recueil des Cours*, 467, 531 (1928).

[14] Jessup, *A Modern Law of Nations*, 99 (1952).

a state is not an international delinquency; even if it were, no state could be empowered to intervene or complain in his behalf because of his lack of nationality.[15]

The absurdity of removing the individual one stage from the application of international law[16] with respect to the responsibility of states for injuries to aliens was summed up by Jessup as follows:

> The responsibility of the state for injuries to an individual is owed under international law to another state and not to the individual. Thus there is no responsibility if the injured individual is stateless, that is, has no nationality. To explain the legal basis of responsibility to another state, international law for some two centuries has made use of a fiction invented by Vattel to the effect that a state is injured through the injury to its citizen. If this were the true basis of responsibility, the measure of damages to be paid for an injury would vary with the importance of the role played by the injured individual in the life of the state of which he is a citizen. Actually, in the hundreds of claims cases which have been adjudicated by international tribunals, lip service only is paid to the fiction, and decisions are made upon the inescapable realization that it is really John Smith or Francis Picaud who has been physically injured or whose widow has been left destitute. The alleged indirect loss to the state is forgotten until the final judgment is expressed in terms of an obligation of the defendant State to pay a sum of money to the claimant State, the usually unexpressed assumption being that the latter will pay the money over to the proper individuals. Many tortuous bits of judicial reasoning would have been eliminated if it were agreed that the individual himself is protected by the rule of law.[17]

It is thus juridically and philosophically unsound to continue to evade the reality that where a procedural safeguard is denied an alien by a host state it is the alien who should be directly protected rather than his state. Accordingly, it is time that the fiction of the injury to the state through the injury to its national be abandoned. The minimum

[15] In the case of the *Panevezys - Saldutiskis Ry., P.C.I.J.* Series A/B, No. 76, 16 (1939) the World Court stated, "...the rule of international law... is that in taking up the case of one of its nationals... a State is in reality asserting its own right, the right to ensure in the person of its nationals respect for the rules of international law. This right is necessarily limited to intervention on behalf of its own nationals because, in the absence of a special agreement, it is the bond of nationality between the State and the individual which alone confers upon the State the right of diplomatic protection, and it is as a part of the function of diplomatic protection that the right to take up a claim and to ensure respect for the rules of international law must be envisaged. Where the injury was done to the national of some other State no claim to which such injury may give rise falls within the scope of the diplomatic protection which a State is entitled to afford nor can it give rise to a claim which that State is entitled to espouse." See 1932 *Annuaire de l'Institut de droit international*, 479 ff, where the rules of the nationality of claims were questioned on the grounds that they reflected the basic artificiality of the law governing the diplomatic protection of citizens abroad. See also Hurst, "Nationality of Claims," 1926 *Brit. Y.B. Int. L.*, 163.

[16] On the basis that the individual is not a "subject" of international law but only an "object."

[17] Jessup, *A Modern Law of Nations* 9 (1952).

procedural safeguards for the protection of an alien who is prosecuted by a host state should be set out in a multilateral convention as direct rights of the alien together with provisions establishing procedures whereby an alien may secure vindication of his rights in the event of a denial thereof.[18]

The minimum procedural safeguards contained in the NATO Status of Forces Agreement and other status of forces agreements are an important precedent which may be utilized in setting out the content of the rights to be accorded an alien in the suggested multilateral convention. They are relatively precise and already have been accepted in the legal systems of the thirteen NATO countries and those of Japan, Nicaragua, Libya, Iceland, the West Indies Federation, and Australia (Nauru Island).[19]

The experience of the United States whose system of law is based on the common law, in the cases of over 4,000 United States servicemen, civilian employees and dependents who during the past eight years have been tried by the tribunals of NATO countries and Japan, whose systems of law are based on the civil law, demonstrates that these safeguards may be successfully applied in two of the major legal systems of the world without substantial disagreement.[20]

As the countries of the Free World to-day are overwhelmingly governed by rules, principles, and institutions stemming from the common or civil law, it is probable that the substance of the safeguards set out in paragraph 9 of Article VII of the NATO Status of Forces Agreement would be acceptable to such countries.[21] Some examples of legal systems influenced by the common or civil law are (1) India, whose legal system was influenced by the common law,[22] (2) Latin-America, whose legal

[18] There is no impediment under traditional international law to this procedure. States by agreement may accord individuals direct rights under international law. The NATO SOF Agreement and other status of forces agreements are instances where aliens have been accorded direct rights to procedural safeguards under international law. These agreements provide that an individual member of the forces of a sending state is entitled to certain rights if he is tried by a receiving state. A further example is the European Convention for the Protection of Human Rights and Fundamental Freedoms which specifically provides that everyone charged with a criminal offense has certain minimum rights (Art. 6(3)).

[19] See Chapter II. It should also be noted that these safeguards have been substantially adopted in Articles 5 and 6 of the *European Convention for the Protection of Human Rights and Fundamental Freedoms*. The text of this convention is set forth in *European Commission on Human Rights, Documents and Decisions*, 1955, 1956, 1957, p. 4 et seq.

[20] See the conclusions of Chapter II.

[21] See Schlesinger, *Comparative Law* (2d ed., 1959) 190–198 for a survey of the geographic expansion of the common and civil law.

[22] See Gledhill, "The Influence of Common Law and Equity on Hindu Law Since 1800," 3 *Int. & Comp. L. Q.* 576 (1954).

systems were influenced by both the common and civil law,[23] (3) Iraq, whose legal systems were influenced by the civil law,[24] and (4) Sudan and Malaya, whose legal systems were influenced by the common law.[25]

Accordingly, as the safeguards enumerated in paragraph 9 of Article VII of the NATO Status of Forces Agreement are clear, are already familiar to a considerable number of states because of their inclusion in Status of Forces Agreements throughout the world, and are likely to be acceptable to countries of all of the major legal systems, it is submitted that they would be an appropriate basis upon which to predicate a minimum standard of procedural justice for all aliens tried by a host country.

Satisfactory as this basis has proved to be, however, it represents a minimum and it should be amplified in the proposed multilateral convention to provide a fuller measure of protection to an alien.

The areas where such improvement could be made are as follows:

(a) The right "to a prompt and speedy trial" requires some amplification. It was previously determined[26] that this right contemplates a prompt and speedy trial in accordance with the law of the host state. If that state is acting in good faith and the delay is legitimate there would be no basis to protest that this right has been denied. Conversely, if it were determined that the delay was due to dilatory or frivolous actions on the part of the authorities of the host state, there would probably be a denial of this right. Accordingly, the words "prompt and speedy" appear to be adequate. An alien, however, who is arrested or detained prior to trial should have some means of testing the lawfulness of his detention. Further, in order to impose a sanction on a host state provision should be made that an alien who has been in arrest or detention and who has been denied a prompt or a speedy trial should have an enforceable right to compensation. This could be accomplished by the following text:

> Whenever an alien is prosecuted under the jurisdiction of a host State he shall be entitled to a prompt and speedy trial. If he is deprived of his liberty by arrest or detention he shall be entitled to take proceedings by which the lawfulness of his detention shall be speedily decided by a court of the host State and his release ordered if the detention is not lawful. Any alien who has been the victim of unlawful arrest or detention or who has been denied a prompt and speedy trial shall have an enforceable right to compensation.

[23] See Eder, "The Impact of the Common Law on Latin America," 4 *Miami L. Q.* 435, 437 (1950).

[24] See Jwaideh, "The New Civil Code of Iraq," 22 *Geo. Wash. L. Rev.* 176, 181 (1953).

[25] See Guttmann, "The Reception of the Common Law in the Sudan," 6 *Int. & Comp. L.Q.* 401 (1957); Buss-Tjen, "Malay Law," 7 *Am. J. Comp. L.* 248 (1958).

[26] See Chapter III.

(b) The right "to be informed, in advance of trial, of the specific charge or charges made against him", should be amplified by the addition of the words "in a language which he understands." This would ensure communication at this stage of the proceedings.

(c) The right "to be confronted with witnesses against him" should be amplified by adding the words "and to have the opportunity to examine them or to have them examined." This would satisfy both the common and civil law examination procedures.[27]

(d) The right "to have compulsory process for obtaining witnesses" in his favour, if they are within the jurisdiction of the host State should be modified by the addition of the words "and their testimony is material." This modification would permit the court to determine the materiality of the testimony.[28]

(e) The right "to have legal representation of his own choice for his defence or to have free or assisted legal representation under the conditions prevailing for the time being in the host State" should be amplified by the addition of the following sentence, "If the law of the host State does not provide free legal representation, an alien, if he has not sufficient means to pay for legal assistance, shall be given it free when the interests of justice so require." This change would assure legal representation in appropriate cases even though it was not provided by the domestic law of the host state.

(f) The right "if he considers it necessary, to have the services of a competent interpreter" should be amplified by the insertion of the word "free" after the words "to have the" and before the words "services of". Further, the words "if he considers it necessary" should be deleted and the words "if he cannot understand or speak the language used in court" should be substituted therefor. The new words would establish an ascertainable criterion for providing an interpreter rather than the unilateral decision of the alien.

(g) The right "to communicate with a representative of the Government of the sending State and, when the rules of the court permit, to have such a representative present at his trial" should be amplified by the addition of the words "at all times" after the first clause. This would insure access to such a representative from the time of the alien's arrest. Further, the words "when the rules of the court permit" should be deleted from the second clause and the words "unless precluded by compelling reasons of national security" added to the end of this clause.

[27] *Ibid.*
[28] *Ibid.*

This change would insure that a representative of the home state of the alien may be present during the trial of sex offenses or offenses by minors from which the public are excluded by the domestic law of many states.[29]

(h) The following right should be added, "An alien shall not be held guilty of a criminal offense on account of any act or omission which did not constitute a criminal offense under national or international law at the time it was committed, and shall not be subject to a greater penalty than the one that was applicable at the time the criminal offense was committed." This safeguard would preclude *ex post facto* offenses and punishments and would enable the alien to rely on the law as it existed contemporaneously with his act or omission.[30]

(i) The following provision should be added, "A High Contracting Party shall secure to every national of another High Contracting Party within its jurisdiction the rights defined in this Convention." This provision would identify those entitled to rights under the Convention and would confirm that they are rights of the alien rather than his state.

Attached as Appendix 4 is a draft of the minimum procedural safeguards to be accorded an alien in such a convention.

In the event the negotiation of this convention is not immediately feasible, it would appear that the United States or any other country should encourage universal adoption of these procedural safeguards by including them in bilateral treaties of friendship, commerce, and navigation.

The NATO SOF Agreement does not contain any procedure by which a member of a force of a sending state could enforce his right to any of the procedural safeguards set out in Article VII in the event of a denial thereof. In such a contingency he must rely on his home state to intervene with the host state in his behalf. Neither under customary international law nor under the agreement does he have any right to compel such intervention.[31]

[29] *Ibid.*

[30] The recent passage of an *ex post facto* law in connection with the "April Revolution Election Riggers," by the Republic of Korea illustrates the desirability of this right. See Korean Law 567. These laws make certain acts criminal which were not criminal when committed, and increased the punishment for certain other criminal acts.

[31] The practice of the United States under the agreement disclosed that although its domestic law did not impose any duty to intervene in such instances, it was especially vigilant in assuring that United States personnel received all of the safeguards in the agreement and that it successfully acted as a bargaining agent for servicemen who had been denied safeguards prescribed in the agreement. Undoubtedly the success of the United States in this respect was due to two factors. One, the NATO SOF Agreement has a functional basis. It was designed to govern the status of the forces of one member of the North Atlantic Treaty Organization when serving in the territory of another. Thus, there was a disposition on the part of host states to favorably consider the repre

It is now proposed to consider the provisions which should be included in the draft multilateral convention to enable an alien to enforce the procedural rights accorded him.

Jessup suggests that if an alien were accorded direct rights under international law it would not be inconsistent to agree that a state may retain the right to represent its national as his agent for collective bargaining.[32] In emphasizing the advantage of such an arrangement Jessup states: "Just as the individual worker is at a bargaining disadvantage in dealing with a great corporation, so the individual traveler or business man or resident alien worker is at a disadvantage in dealing with a foreign government."[33]

A provision in the draft multilateral convention entitling the home state to represent its national who has been denied a right accorded to him would continue the traditional international practice of the home state of the alien dealing directly with the host state but on the new and more valid basis of being an agent for the alien. It would have the practical effect of securing for the individual all of the advantages enjoyed by his state by virtue of its being a continuing participant in the international arena. In this way the alien would benefit by the interaction of his state with and upon other states in their pursuit of common community goals. The successful experience of the NATO countries in the implementation of the "fair trial" safeguards illustrates the importance of this mutuality of interest. This provision, however, would leave the alien without a remedy if his home state refused to act as his agent.

Another way to assure that an alien may enforce a direct right granted to him by the proposed convention is the establishment of an international body to which he could petition in the event of a denial of such rights. At present there does not exist any international tribunal to which an alien could petition directly for the enforcement of any procedural rights accorded to him by the contemplated multilateral convention.

Precedent for the inclusion of such a provision in a multilateral agreement pertaining to minimum procedural safeguards, however, is con-

sentations of United States authorities as to the denial of a procedural safeguard set out in Article VII of the Agreement by a receiving state in the prosecution of a United States serviceman. Two, the stature of the United States as a major power also enhanced its bargaining power in such negotiations.

[32] Jessup, *A Modern Law of Nations*, 116 (1952).

[33] *Id.* at 116, 117.

[34] See *European Commission of Human Rights, Documents and Decisions* 4 (1955, 1956, 1957) for the text of this convention.

tained in the Convention for the Protection of Human Rights and Fundamental Freedoms.[34] This agreement provides that individuals may petition the European Commission of Human Rights in cases where a member state has violated one of the rights set out in the Convention, if the state concerned has recognized the competence of the Commission to receive such petitions.

In substance the procedure established with respect to such petitions is as follows:

The Commission may receive petitions from any person, non-governmental organization or group of individuals claiming to be the victim of a violation by one of the High Contracting Parties of the rights set forth in the Convention.[35] The Commission, however, may deal with the matter only after all domestic remedies have been exhausted, according to the generally recognized rules of international law and within a period of six months from the date on which the final action was taken.[36] The Commission has the right to accept or reject the petition.[37] If it accept the petition it will attempt to effect a friendly settlement between the parties concerned.[38] If such a solution is not reached, it will prepare a full report on the case and will include therein its opinion as to whether the facts found disclose a breach on the part of the state concerned. This report will be transmitted to the Committee of Ministers, together with any proposals the Committee thinks appropriate.[39] If none of the eligible High Contracting Parties or the Commission[40] bring the case before the European Court of Human Rights [41] during the three months from the date of the transmission of the Report of the Committee of Ministers, the Committee of Ministers shall decide by a majority of two-thirds whether there has been a violation of the Convention.[42] If it decides there has been a violation, the Committee will prescribe a period during which the High Contracting Party concerned must take the measures required by the Committee of Ministers. On the other hand, if the case is referred to the Court, the judgment of the Court is final and the High Contracting Parties who are parties undertake to abide by the decision.[43] In the event of noncompliance the High

[35] Art. 25.
[36] Art. 26
[37] Art. 27.
[38] Art. 28.
[39] Art. 31.
[40] Art. 48.
[41] Art. 38 *et seq.*
[42] Art. 32.
[43] Arts. 50–53.

Contracting Party may be asked to withdraw from the Council of Europe or may be removed from membership by the Committee of Ministers.[44]

Thus, the *Convention for the Protection of Human Rights and Fundamental Freedoms* provides the essential ingredients for an orderly and expeditious disposal of cases where the right of an individual which has been provided by the Convention has been violated.

Although a modified version of these procedures could be included in a multilateral convention designed to provide minimum procedural safeguards for aliens, the concept of allowing an individual to enforce his right to such safeguards directly against a host state fails to recognize the realities of the present day international arena. Such procedures would be a radical departure from traditional international practice and would infringe upon the sovereignty of states. Consequently, while states may agree to accord aliens the right to minimum procedural safeguards, they probably would be extremely reluctant to permit aliens to enforce their rights directly against a state. It is doubtful whether the agreement of all or even a substantial number of states could be obtained to inserting such a provision in the proposed multilateral convention. The formulation of such procedures *de lege ferranda*, however, would be most desirable.

As neither of the two provisions discussed above are by themselves satisfactory, it is suggested that a combination of them would best provide the alien with adequate procedures to enforce his right to the minimum procedural safeguards contained in the proposed multilateral convention. Such a provision should provide first, that the home state of the alien may represent him as his agent in the manner heretofore discussed and secondly, that in the event the home state of the alien refuses to so enforce a right accorded to him under the convention, the alien would be entitled to proceed directly against the host state to effect a friendly settlement. While this latter clause may be objected to by a number of states, a serious attempt should be made to include it in the draft multilateral convention. Otherwise, an alien would be powerless to enforce a right if his home state refused to espouse his cause.

Any provision included in such a convention entitling the home state of the alien or, alternatively, the alien, to enforce his right to the procedural safeguards contained therein should state a specific period of

[44] Art. 8, Statute of the Council of Europe, signed at London on 5 May 1949. See *European Commission of Human Rights, Documents and Decisions*, 4 (1955, 1956, 1957) for the text of this article.

time within which the home state or the alien may intervene directly with the host state which has allegedly denied the safeguard in an attempt to reach a friendly settlement. It is especially important to inject a time limit as to the initiation of claims in order to avoid abnormal delays. If a friendly settlement is not then obtained, the home state or the alien should be entitled to proceed against the host state before an international tribunal specified by the states signatory to the convention as having jurisdiction over the matter.

The Convention should also provide that the procedures for enforcing the right of an alien to a particular procedural safeguard may not be employed until all domestic remedies provided by the host state have been exhausted, according to the generally recognized rules of international law.

A draft of an article setting out the above is attached at Appendix 5.

It should be noted that the enforcement of a right to a procedural safeguard by an alien does not necessarily mean claiming monetary damages for the denial of such a right. In many cases it will mean providing a new trial, setting aside his conviction or otherwise airing the denial by further judicial proceedings or by the authorities of the host state. If it is impossible for the host state to correct the denial of the procedural safeguard, such as in cases of unlawful confinement, the alien would then be entitled to claim monetary damages in compensation.

A criticism of this procedure might be that it provides no effective sanctions against those states who violate the obligations they have assumed under the multilateral convention. It is believed, however, that if a state commits itself formally to abide by the decision of the International Tribunal provided in the convention, there will be almost universal compliance. This belief is based on the fact that the record of international adjudication reveals relatively few cases of noncompliance. In the sixty-odd decisions of the Permanent Court of International Justice there was no case of a refusal to comply.[45] In the Inter-

[45] See Hudson, *The Permanent Court of International Justice* (2d ed., 1943), p. 596. But not all decisions were fully carried out. In the *Wimbledon* case, *P.C.I.J.* Series A. No. 1 (1923), the decision of the court in favor of Germany was not carried out, since the Reparations Commission, of which France was a member, held that the damage should not be paid. This inability was reported to the court by the German Minister at the Hague, but there was no public pronouncement about it. In the *Société Commercial de Belgique* case, *P.C.I.J.* A/B-78 (1939), the Court held that the awards made against Greece in an arbitration award of 1936 were binding. These awards were still unpaid in 1950. See *Summarization of Socobelge and the Belgium State* v. *Kingdom of the Hellenes*, 47 *A.J.I.L.* 508 (1953). See also *Proceedings Second Summer Conference on International Law*, Cornell Law School, Ithaca, New York, June 23–25, 1958 at page 103.

national Court of Justice there has been only one case of noncompliance, the failure of Albania to pay the damages awarded to the United Kingdom in the CORFU channel case.[46] In arbitration, too, noncompliance has been comparatively rare. There are not more than a few cases out of many hundreds which have involved the refusal by the losing party to give effect to an award rendered.[47]

It is now proposed to return to the hypothetical case set out previously in this chapter. In that case it was determined that under traditional international law the alien, who had been denied an interpreter during his trial by the host state, had to rely on his home state to obtain a somewhat uncertain redress from the host state. What remedies would the alien have if the draft multilateral convention had been in effect at the time of this trial?

The draft multilateral convention grants the alien a limited international personality. Under it he is accorded various procedural safeguards as direct personal rights. As a consequence of this limited international personality he would have had in the hypothetical case a right to the free services of a competent interpreter if he could not speak or understand the language of the host country. (See par 1f, Appendix 4). Thus, the denial by the host country of an interpreter in the hypothetical case would be a clear violation of the draft multilateral convention and the alien would not be prejudiced by the lack of any customary rule of international law setting forth this right. Further, upon the denial of his right to an interpreter, the draft multilateral conven-

[46] See *I.C.J. Pleadings* (1954) in *Monetary Gold* case (Italy v. France, United Kingdom and United States) per Sir Gerald Fitzmaurice at p. 126:

> Eight months later, that is to say, on December 15, 1949, and therefore about four and a half years ago, the court gave a further decision in which, by the large majority of 12 votes to 2, it gave judgement in favour of the United Kingdom's claim to damages, and fixed the amount of compensation due from the People's Republic of Albania to the United Kingdom..., in terms of dollars, at a sum of approximately two and a half millions.
>
> Not a penny of these damages, fixed more than four years go, has in fact been paid, and I believe I am right in saying that this constitutes almost the only case in which a decision (at any rate a final decision) whether of this court or of its predecessor, has not eventually been complied with by the country against which it was given.

[47] See La Fontaine, "Histoire Sommaire et Chronologique des Arbitrages Internationaux," 1902 *Revue de Droit International*, 349, 558, 622. In the period 1794–1900 Hambro, *L'Exécution des sentences internationales* (Liège, 1936), was only able to find 20 cases where the possibility of noncompliance even existed. See also La Pradelle, "De l'exécution de la justice," 14 *Revue de Droit International* (1934), p. 225; Secretariat Commentary on the Draft Convention on Arbitral Procedure, *U.N. Doc.* A/CN. 4/92 at p. 92; and Jessup, *A Modern Law of Nations*, 6 (1952). See Hudson in *International Tribunals* 129 (1944) who states, "It is a striking fact that States have seldom refused to carry out or abide by the decisions of international tribunals."

tion sets out a precise step by step procedure to be followed by the alien to enforce his right. (See Appendix 5).

Under this procedure the home state of the alien may intervene directly with the host state. The home state, however, is not intervening in its own behalf, as was the case under traditional international law, but rather in behalf of the alien as his agent. This intervention must be within six months of the final action on the alien's case by the host country. If a settlement is not reached as a result of these bilateral negotiations, the home state of the alien is entitled to proceed against the host state before the international tribunal provided in the convention. The decision of this tribunal is final and binding upon all the parties. In the event the home of the alien refuses to intervene in his behalf, the alien is then entitled to attempt to effect a friendly settlement by presenting his complaint directly to the offending state. Failing such a settlement, he may personally present his complaint against the offending state to the international tribunal provided by the convention whose decision will be final and binding upon all parties.

In consequence of the procedures set out in the draft multilateral convention the alien in the hypothetical case is in an enormously more advantageous position than he was under traditional international law to remedy the denial of an interpreter at his trial by the host state. Additionally, he would have a right to the other procedural safeguards in the draft multilateral convention and the opportunity to enforce such rights.

The draft multilateral convention proposed above is a means of resolving the existing controversy in international law as to the minimum procedural safeguards a host country must accord in the prosecution of an alien. Once the agreement of states has been obtained to such a convention there should emerge eventually from the interaction of states, each upon the other, in the reciprocal implementation of these safeguards a common denominator as to their meaning. This decision making process should be accelerated by the fact that peoples everywhere are interdependent with respect to major values. In recent decades tremendous and sweeping changes in technology, transportation, population growth and movement, educational opportunities, economic development, and world organization have combined to alter the status of the nations of the world from one of comparative independence to one of ever increasing interdependence. This interdependence and the ever increasing acceptance of common community economic goals should encourage a nation signatory to the multilateral convention to accord in the prosecution of an alien the minimum procedural safeguards contained therein in the expectation that such procedure will maximize the opportunity of its nationals abroad being similarly treated by other states. Thus, through this informal approach there should be, even among nations having different legal systems and cultures, mutual agreement as to the meaning of the safeguards to be accorded aliens under the proposed multilateral convention.

At this time these procedural safeguards will be ripe for codification into a binding and enforceable bill of procedural rights, not just for aliens, but for all mankind.

The proposed convention, if adopted, would truly represent a pragmatic step in the realm of reality toward the achievement of a common standard in the area of minimum procedural rights "for all people of all nations" as contemplated by the abstract ideals of the *Universal Declaration of Human Rights.*

CHAPTER VI

SUMMARY OF RECOMMENDATIONS

The absence of any major controversy between the United States and those nations having different legal systems and cultures in the implementation of the NATO "fair trial" safeguards in literally thousands of cases during the past eight years has been largely the result of the desire of the decision-makers of the nations concerned to achieve the common goal of mutual defense. As a consequence, the defensive alliance of NATO has generated, in the implementation of the NATO "fair trial" safeguards, a further bond among the signatories by demonstrating that even differences in their legal systems may be successfully accommodated. Through an informal approach these nations have interacted with and upon each other in a social and decision making process to shape desirable community prescriptions to promote their common goal. This practical application of the NATO "fair trial" safeguards, in addition to demonstrating the community decision making process in action, also represents a unique breakthrough in the implementation of human rights. In consonance with the main purpose of this inquiry a course of action has been recommended by which the practice of the United States and other nations in the implementation of the SOF "fair trial" safeguards in different systems of law may be utilized in an informal approach to achieve in one small area of human rights where there is disagreement among nations an orderly modification of international law, which would lead ultimately to the universal acceptance of such rights in an international Bill of Procedural Rights.

The area chosen was the minimum procedural safeguards to be accorded an alien prosecuted by a host country. It has been demonstrated that in this area there is a dichotomy among groups of nations as to the criteria to be applied in determining such safeguards. One substantial group of states adheres to the "national treatment" theory and urges that a host state is only required to provide in the prosecution of an alien those procedural safeguards which they accord their own nationals.

Another equally substantial group of states advocates the "minimum standard" theory and asserts that a host state must accord an alien prosecuted in its courts those procedural safeguards which are prescribed by the minimum standard of procedural justice. In consequence of this dichotomy among nations there was never established any customary rule of international law which established the minimum procedural safeguards which a host state must accord an alien who is prosecuted in its courts. Further, there is serious doubt that either the "national treatment" theory or the "minimum standard" theory will ever be accepted as a rule of international law. Even if so accepted, it is questionable whether either theory provides criteria which would assure uniform safeguards in the trial of aliens by different countries. The "national treatment" theory by its nature will vary from state to state and the "minimum standard" theory lacks precision and is a hopeless failure as a definitive norm. It was concluded that if aliens prosecuted in a court of a host state are to be accorded uniform procedural safeguards a basis other than the "national treatment" theory or the "minimum standard" theory is needed. It was suggested that once such a basis was formulated it could be included in a universal multilateral convention and would thus nullify the current controversy between the "national treatment" states and the "minimum standard" states. It was recommended that such safeguards should be set out in a multilateral convention as direct rights of the alien rather than as rights of his state and that procedures should be provided whereby an alien may secure vindication of his rights in the event of a denial thereof. The minimum procedural safeguards contained in the NATO and other status of forces agreements are an important precedent which may be utilized in establishing a mutually agreeable basis among states as to what procedural rights should be accorded an alien prosecuted by a host country. They are relatively precise and already have been accepted by the legal systems of the 13 NATO countries and those of Japan, Pakistan, Nicaragua, Libya, Iceland, the West Indies Federation, and Australia (Nauru Islands).

As the countries of the Free World to-day are overwhelmingly governed by rules, principles, and institutions stemming from the civil and common law it is probable that the substance of the safeguards set out in the NATO Status of Forces Agreement would be acceptable to countries utilizing these systems. Attached as Appendix 4 is a draft of minimum procedural safeguards to be accorded by a host state in the prosecution of an alien. It was recommended that these safeguards be utilized in the proposed multilateral convention. In the event such a convention is not immediately feasible, it was recommended that the United States or any other country should encourage universal adoption of these procedural safeguards for aliens by including them in bilateral treaties of friendship, commerce, and navigation. It was also recommended that an effective way to assure that an alien may enforce a direct right granted to him by the proposed convention was to entitle the home state of the alien to represent him on the new and more valid basis of agency. (See Appendix 5).

It is believed that the informal reciprocal decision making process which was so successful in the implementation of the NATO "fair trial" safeguards will in time establish among nations having different legal systems a common denominator as to the substance and meaning of each procedural right. This process will be accelerated by the ever increasing interdependence of nations and by their ever increasing acceptance of mutual community goals. Once this common denominator has been formalized, the procedural rights in issue would then be ripe for codification in a binding and enforceable Bill of Procedural Rights for all persons which would contribute to raising and safeguarding the status of man in the international legal system.

With respect to the subordinate purpose of this inquiry it was concluded that although a United States serviceman has been accorded under international law a right to the NATO "fair trial" safeguards, he has not been provided any procedural capacity under international law by which he himself may enforce this right. In the event of a denial of a "fair trial" safeguard the serviceman under international law must rely on the United States to intervene with the host state to protect his right. Further, under United States domestic law if the Secretary of State refused to intervene, the Federal courts would probably not compel such intervention, as negotiation with a foreign state is not a ministerial duty. Consequently, from the viewpoint of the serviceman the "fair trial" safeguards accorded him by the various SOF agreements are somewhat meaningless as he lacks the capacity to enforce them himself. He possesses at most a passive or inchoate right to the "fair trial" safeguards set out in these agreements. In this respect the draft multilateral convention provides that in the event the home state of an alien refuses to enforce his rights, the alien may proceed against the offending host state in his own right. (See pars 3 and 4, Appendix 5).

Appendix 1

RESOLUTION OF RATIFICATION, WITH RESERVATIONS, AS AGREED TO BY THE SENATE ON JULY 15, 1953

Resolved (two-thirds of the Senators present concurring therein), That the Senate advise and consent to the ratification of Executive T, Eighty-second Congress, second session, an agreement between the parties to the North Atlantic Treaty Regarding the Status of their Forces, signed at London on June 19, 1951.

It is the understanding of the Senate, which understanding inheres in its advice and consent to the ratification of the Agreement, that nothing in the Agreement diminishes, abridges, or alters the right of the United States of America to safeguard its own security by excluding or removing persons whose presence in the United States is deemed prejudicial to its safety or security, and that no person whose presence in the United States is deemed prejudicial to its safety or security shall be permitted to enter or remain in the United States.

In giving its advice and consent to ratification, it is the sense of the Senate that:

(1) The criminal jurisdiction provisions of Article VII do not constitute a precedent for future agreements;

(2) Where a person subject to the military jurisdiction of the United States is to be tried by the authorities of a receiving state, under the treaty the commanding officer of the armed forces of the United States in such state shall examine the laws of such state with particular reference to the procedural safeguards contained in the Constitution of the United States;

(3) If, in the opinion of such commanding officer, under all the circumstances of the case, there is danger that the accused will not be protected because of the absence or denial of constitutional rights he would enjoy in the United States, the commanding officer shall request the authorities of the receiving state to waive jurisdiction in accordance with the provisions of paragraph 3(c) of Article VII (which requires the receiving state to give "sympathetic consideration" to such request) and if such authorities refuse to waive jurisdiction, the commanding officer shall request the Department of State to press such request through diplomatic channels and notification shall be given by the Executive Branch to the Armed Services Committees of the Senate and House of Representatives;

(4) A representative of the United States to be appointed by the Chief of Diplomatic Mission with the advice of the senior United States military representative in the receiving state will attend the trial of any such person by the authorities of a receiving state under the agreement, and any failure to comply with the provisions of paragraph 9 of Article VII of the agreement shall be reported to the commanding officer of the armed forces of the United States in such state who shall then request the Department of State to take appropriate action to protect the rights of the accused, and notification shall be given by the

Executive Branch to the Armed Services Committee of the Senate and House of Representatives.

Appendix 2

FORMAT OF OBSERVER REPORT

(1) Name, grade (if applicable), service number (if applicable), organization (if applicable), home address, of the accused.
(2) Offense(s) charged. (Brief statement) Date and place of alleged offense.
(3) Name, location and type of court.
(4) Date(s) and place(s) of trial.
(5) Conviction, acquittal, or charges dropped.
If convicted, offense(s) of which convicted.
(6) Sentence: (Reprimand, Fine, Confinement) suspended, not suspended, or stayed pending appeal.
(7) Appeal by accused or prosecution. (If known in time for a timely submission of the observer's report; if not, a later separate report on whether an appeal has been taken should be sent.)
(8) Text of allegations of complaint.
(9) Citation and text of statutes involved.
(10) Defense counsel
- employed by accused or appointed by court or refused by accused or US Government supplied.
- adequacy (include whether English-speaking).
(11) Interpreter(s)
- employed by accused or appointed by court or US Government supplied.
- adequacy.
(12) Resume of trial proceedings.
(13) Comment on fairness of trial, with especial emphasis on observance of procedural safeguards guaranteed by international agreement.
(14) Signature(s) of observer(s) attending trial.

Appendix 3

ARTICLE VII, NATO SOF AGREEMENT

1. Subject to the provisions of this Article,

a. the military authorities of the sending State shall have the right to exercise within the receiving State all criminal and disciplinary jurisdiction conferred on them by the law of the sending State over all persons subject to the military law of that State;

b. the authorities of the receiving State shall have jurisdiction over the members of a force or civilian component and their dependents with respect to offences committed within the territory of the receiving State and punishable by the law of that State.

2.–*a.* The military authorities of the sending State shall have the right to exercise exclusive jurisdiction over persons subject to the military law of that State with respect to offences, including offences relating to its security, punishable by the law of the sending State, but not by the law of the receiving State.

b. The authorities of the receiving State shall have the right to exercise exclusive jurisdiction over members of a force or civilian component and their dependents with respect to offences, including offences relating to the security of that State, punishable by its law but not by the law of the sending State.

c. For the purposes of this paragraph and of paragraph 3 of this Article a security offence against a State shall include

(i) treason against the State;

(ii) sabotage, espionage or violation of any law relating to official secrets of that State, or secrets relating to the national defence of that State.

3. In cases where the right to exercise jurisdiction is concurrent the following rules shall apply:

a. The military authorities of the sending State shall have the primary right to exercise jurisdiction over a member of a force or of a civilian component in relation to

(i) offences solely against the property or security of that State, or offences solely against the person or property of another member of the force or civilian component of that State or of a dependent;

(ii) offences arising out of any act or omission done in the performance of official duty.

b. In the case of any other offence the authorities of the receiving State shall have the primary right to exercise jurisdiction.

c. If the State having the primary right decides not to exercise jurisdiction, it shall notify the authorities of the other State as soon as practicable. The authorities of the State having the primary right shall give sympathetic consideration to a request from the authorities of the other State for a waiver of its right in cases where that other State considers such waiver to be of particular importance.

4. The foregoing provisions of this Article shall not imply any right for the military authorities of the sending State to exercise jurisdiction over persons who are nationals of or ordinarily resident in the receiving State, unless they are members of the force of the sending State.

5.–*a.* The authorities of the receiving and sending States shall assist each other in the arrest of members of a force or civilian component or their dependents in the territory of the receiving State and in handing them over to the authority which is to exercise jurisdiction in accordance with the above provisions.

b. The authorities of the receiving State shall notify promptly the military authorities of the sending State of the arrest of any member of a force or civilian component or a dependent.

c. The custody of an accused member of a force or civilian component over whom the receiving State is to exercise jurisdiction shall, if he is in the hands of the sending State, remain with that State until he is charged by the receiving State.

6.–*a.* The authorities of the receiving and sending States shall assist each other in the carrying out of all necessary investigations into offences, and in the collection and production of evidence, including the seizure and, in proper cases, the handing over of objects connected with an offence. The handing over of such objects may, however, be made subject to their return within the time specified by the authority delivering them.

b. The authorities of the Contracting Parties shall notify one another of the disposition of all cases in which there are concurrent rights to exercise jurisdiction.

7.–*a.* A death sentence shall not be carried out in the receiving State by the authorities of the sending State if the legislation of the receiving State does not provide for such punishment in a similar case.

b. The authorities of the receiving State shall give sympathetic consideration to a request from the authorities of the sending State for assistance in carrying out a sentence of imprisonment pronounced by the authorities of the sending State under the provision of this Article within the territory of the receiving State.

8. Where an accused has been tried in accordance with the provisions of this Article by the authorities of one Contracting Party and has been acquitted, or has been convicted and is serving, or has served, his sentence or has been pardoned, he may not be tried again for the same offence within the same territory by the authorities of another Contracting Party. However, nothing in this paragraph shall prevent the military authorities of the sending State from trying a member of its force for any violation of rules of discipline arising from an act or omission which constituted an offence for which he was tried by the authorities of another Contracting Party.

9. Whenever a member of a force or civilian component or a dependent is prosecuted under the jurisdiction of a receiving State he shall be entitled:

a. to a prompt and speedy trial;

b. to be informed, in advance of trial, of the specific charge or charges made against him.

c. to be confronted with the witnesses against him;

d. to have compulsory process for obtaining witnesses, in his favour, if they are within the jurisdiction of the receiving State;

e. to have legal representation of his own choice for his defence or to have free or assisted legal representation under the conditions prevailing for the time being in the receiving State;

f. if he considers it necessary, to have the services of a competent interpreter; and

g. to communicate with a representative of the Government of the sending State, and when the rules of the court permit, to have such a representative present at his trial.

10.–*a.* Regularly constituted military units or formations of a force shall have the right to police any camps, establishments or other premises which they occupy as the result of an agreement with the receiving State. The military police of the force may take all appropriate measures to ensure the maintenance of order and security on such premises.

b. Outside these premises, such military police shall be employed only subject to arrangements with the authorities of the receiving State and in liaison with those authorities, and in so far as such employment is necessary to maintain discipline and order among the members of the force.

11. Each Contracting Party shall seek such legislation as it deems necessary to ensure the adequate security and protection within its territory of installations, equipment, property, records and official information of other Contracting Parties, and the punishment of persons who may contravene laws enacted for that purpose.

Appendix 4

MINIMUM PROCEDURAL SAFEGUARDS TO BE ACCORDED ALIENS

1. Whenever an alien is prosecuted under the jurisdiction of a host State he shall have the following rights:

a. To a prompt and speedy trial. If he is deprived of his liberty by arrest or detention he shall be entitled to take proceedings by which the lawfulness of his detention shall be speedily decided by a court of the host State and his release ordered if the detention is not lawful. Any alien who has been the victim of unlawful arrest or detention or who has been denied a prompt and speedy trial shall have an enforceable right to compensation.

b. To be informed in advance of trial, of the specific charge or charges made against him in a language which he understands.

c. To be confronted with witnesses against him and to have the opportunity to examine them or to have them examined.

d. To have compulsory process for obtaining witnesses in his favour, if they are within the jurisdiction of the host State and their testimony is material.

e. To have legal representation of his own choice for his defense or to have free or assisted legal representation under the conditions prevailing for the time being in the host State. If the law of the host State, however, does not provide free legal representation, an alien, if he has not sufficient means to pay for legal assistance shall be given it free when the interest of justice so require.

f. To have, if he cannot understand or speak the language used in court, the free services of a competent interpreter, at all stages of the proceedings.

g. To communicate with a representative of his State at all times and to have such a representative present at his trial unless precluded by compelling reasons of national security of the host State.

2. An alien shall not be held guilty of a criminal offense on account of any act or omission which did not constitute a criminal offense under national or international law at the time it was committed, and shall not be subject to a heavier penalty than the one that was applicable at the time the criminal offense was committed.

3. A High Contracting Party shall secure to every national of another High Contracting Party within its jurisdiction the rights defined in this convention.

4. An alien may at any time waive his right to any procedural safeguard set out in this Article.

Appendix 5

PROCEDURE WHERE A RIGHT HAS BEEN DENIED

1. In the event of a denial by a signatory of a right accorded an alien by this convention a state is entitled to intervene on behalf of its national directly with the state which is alleged to be responsible within a period of six months from the time the final action was taken to effect a friendly settlement.

2. If such a settlement is not reached, the state which is acting on behalf of its national is entitled to proceed against the other state before an international tribunal as provided in Article ... of this Convention. The decision of the international tribunal will be final and binding upon all parties.

3. In the event the home state of the alien refuses to intervene in his behalf with a state which has allegedly denied a right to the alien, the alien in order to effect a friendly settlement is entitled to present his complaint directly to the state alleged to be responsible within a period of six months from the time the final action was taken.

4. If after the presentation of the above complaint, the matter is not settled the alien may present his complaint to the international tribunal provided by Article ... of this Convention. The decision of the international tribunal will be final and binding upon all parties.

5. The above procedures may not be utilized until all of the domestic remedies provided by the host state have been exhausted, according to the generally recognized rules of international law. The term "final action" as used in paragraphs 1 and 3, above, refers to that action which exhausts the domestic remedies provided by the host state under the generally recognized rules of international law.

6. Under extraordinary conditions, not within the control of the home state of the alien or the alien, the international tribunal provided in Article ... of this Convention may waive the six months restriction provided in this article.

BIBLIOGRAPHY

ARTICLES AND PERIODICALS

Barton, "Foreign Armed Forces; Immunity from Criminal Jurisdiction," 27 *Brit. Y. B. Int'l L.*, 186 (1950).

Beckett, *Grotius Society*, Vol. 17, 175 (1932).

Borchard, *Annuaire de l'Institut de Droit International* (1931) 55.

– , "The 'Minimum Standard' of the Treatment of Aliens," *Proceedings of A. J. I. L. at its 33rd meeting* (1939) 55.

Brierly, "Le Fondement de Caractère obligatoire du droit international." 23 *Recueil des cours*, 467, 531 (1928).

Buss-Tjen, "Malay Law," 7 *Am. J. Comp. L.* 248 (1958).

Cavaglieri, *Recueil des cours*, Vol. 26 (1929 I) 456.

Dunn, "The International Rights of Individuals," 1941 *Am. Soc. Int. L. Proc.* 14.

Eder, "The Impact of the Common Law on Latin America," 4 *Miami L. Q.* 435, 437 (1950).

Ellert, "The United States as a Receiving State," 63 *Dickinson Law Review* 75.

Fenwick, "Intervention: Individual and Collective." 39 *A. J. I. L.* 645 (1945).

Fitzmaurice, "The Meaning of the Term Denial of Justice," 13 *Brit. Y. B. Int'l L.*, 100–101 (1932).

Freeman, "Recent Aspects of the Calvo Doctrine and the Challenge to International Law," 40 *A. J. I. L.* 132.

García, "State Responsibility Some New Problems," *Recueil des cours*, 369, 1958 II (Vol. 94).

Garner, "Executive Discretion in the Conduct of Foreign Relations, "31 *A. J. I. L.* 289 (1937).

Gledhill, "The Influence of Common Law and Equity on Hindu Law since 1800," 3 *Int. &* Comp. *L. Q.* 576 (1954).

Guttman, "The Reception of the Common Law in the Sudan," 6 *Int. & Comp. L. Q.* 401 (1957).

Hudson, "The First Conference For the Codification of International Law," 24 *A. J. I. L.* 460 (1930).

Hurst, "Nationality of Claims," 1926 *Brit. Y. B. Int'l L.* 163.

Jwaideh, "The New Civil Code of Iraq," 22 *Geo. Wash. L. Rev.* 176, 181 (1953).

King, "Jurisdiction Over Friendly Armed Forces," 36 *Am. L. Int'l J.* 539.

– , "Further Developments Concerning Jurisdiction Over Friendly Foreign Armed Forces," 40 *Am. J. Int'l L.* 257 (1944).

La Fontaine, "Histoire Sommaire et Chronologique des Arbitrages Internationaux," 1902 *Revue de Droit International*, 349, 558.

Levie, "Some Legal Problems Arising Under the NATO Status of Forces Agreement and the Administrative Agreement with Japan," 17 *Fed. B. J.* 620 (1957).

McDougal, "International Law, Power and Policy: A Contemporary Conception," *Recueil des cours* (1953) Vol. I, 140.

Note, "Criminal Jurisdiction Over American Armed Forces Abroad," 70 *Harv. L. Rev.*, 1043, 1957.
Parry, "Some Considerations Upon the Protection of Individuals in International Law," *Recueil des cours*, 1956, II, Vol. 90, 42.
Pradelle, "De L'exécution de la Justice," 14 *Revue de Droit International* (1934) 225.
Scelle, Revue Générale de Droit International Public, *R. G. D. I. P.*, Vol. 34 (1927) 464–465.
Schuck, "Concurrent Jurisdiction Under the NATO Status of Forces Agreement," 57 *Colum. L. Rev.* 355 (1957).
Schwartz, "International Law and the NATO Status of Forces Agreement," 53 *Colum. L. Rev.* 1091 (1953).
Summarization of Socobelge and the Belgium State v. Kingdom of the Hellenes, 47 *A. J. I. L.* 508 (1953).
Verdross, *Recueil des cours*, Vol. 37 (1931 111) 353–357.

BOOKS

Alvarez, *Le Droit International Américain* (Paris), 1910.
Berdahl, *The War Powers of the Executive in the U. S.*, (1920).
Borchard, *The Diplomatic Protection of Citizens Abroad*, (1951).
Briggs, *The Law of Nations, Cases, Documents and Notes*, (1952).
Byrd, *Treaties and Executive Agreements in the U. S.*, (1960).
Calvo, *Le Droit International* (Paris) (5th ed. 1896).
Corwin, *The President*, (1957).
– , *The President's Control of Foreign Relations*, (1922).
Dunn, *The Protection of Nationals*, (1932).
Eagelton, *The Responsibility of States*, (1928).
Fenwick, *International Law*, (3d ed. 1948).
Freeman, *Denial of Justice*, (1938).
Friedman, *Legal Theory*, (3d ed. 1953).
Hackworth, *Digest of International Law*.
Hambro, *L'Exécution des sentences internationales*, (Liège, 1936).
Hudson, *International Tribunals Past and Future*, (1944).
– , *The Permanent Court of International Justice*, (2d ed. 1943).
Jessup, *A Modern Law of Nations*, (1952).
– , *The Use of International Law*, (1959).
– , *Transnational Law*, (1956).
Korowicz, *Introduction to International Law*, (1959).
Lauterpacht, *International Law and Human Rights*, (1950).
McDougal and Associates, *Studies in World Public Order*, (1960).
Oppenheim, *International Law* (8th ed., Lauterpacht 1955).
Pomeroy, *Constitutional Law*, (1888).
Ralston, *The Law and Procedure of International Tribunals*, (1926).
Roth, *The Minimum Standard of International Justice Applied to Aliens* Leiden (1949).
Schlesinger, *Comparative Law* (2d ed. 1959).
Schwarzenberger, International Law, Vol. 1, *International Law As Applied by International Courts and Tribunals* 1 (3d ed. 1957).
Snee and Pye, *Status of Forces Agreement: Criminal Jurisdiction*, (1957).
Vattel, *Le Droit Des Gens*, Book II.
Wigmore Evidence (3d ed. 1940).

CASES

WORLD COURT

Asylum Case I. C. J. Reports (1950) 266.
Chorzow Factory Case, P. C. I. J. (1928) Series A, No, 17.
Interhandel Case, I. C. J. Reports (1959) 27.
Mavrommatis Palestine Concession Case, P. C. I. J. (1924) Series A, No. 2.
Nottebohm (Second Phase) Case, I. C. J. Reports (1955) 24.
Peter Pazmany University Case, P. C. I. J. Series A/B, No. 61, 231.
Panevezys – Saldutiskis Ry. Case, P. C. I. J. Series A/B No. 76, 16 (1939).
Rights of U. S. Nationals Case, I. C. J. Reports (1952) 200.
Société Commerciale de Belgique Case, P. C. I. J. Series A/B, No. 78 (1939).
Wimbledon case, P. C. I. J. Series A, No. 1 (1923).

SUPREME COURT OF UNITED STATES

Barron use of Tiernan v. *Baltimore,* 7 Pet. 243 (1833).
Beavers v. *Haubert,* 198 U.S. 77, 87.
Decatur v. *Paulding,* 14 Pet. 497 (1840).
Grisham v. *Hagan,* 361 U.S. 278.
Head Money Cases, 112 U.S. 589, 598 (1884).
Kendal v. *U.S.,* 12 Pet. 524 (1838).
Kinsella v. *Singleton,* 361 U.S. 234 (1960).
Kirby v. *United States,* 174 U. S. 47 (1809).
Marbury v. *Madison,* 1 Cr. 137 (1803).
McElroy v. *Guagliardo,* 361 U.S. 281 (1960).
Mattox v. *United States,* 156 U.S. 237, 240 (1895).
Ness v. *Fisher,* 223 U.S. 683 (1912).
Pollard v. *United States,* 352 U.S. 354 (1957).
Reid v. *Covert,* 354 U.S. 1 (1957).
Riverside Oil Co. v. *Hitchcock,* 190 U.S. 316 (1903).
Salinger v. *United States,* 272 U.S. 542 (1926).
U.S. ex rel Dunlap v. *Block,* 128 U.S. 40 (1888).
U.S. v. *Curtiss-Wright Export Corporation,* 299 U.S. 304 (1936).
U.S. ex rel Carrick v. *Lamar,* 116 U.S. 423 (1886).
U.S. ex rel International Contracting Company v. *Lamont,* 155 U.S. 303, 308 (1894).
U.S. v. *MacVeagh,* 214 U.S. 124 (1909).
United States v. *Schurz,* 102 U.S. 378 (1880).
Ware v. *Hylton,* 3 Dall. 199 (1796).
Wilbur v. *U.S. ex rel Kadrie,* 281 U.S. 206 (1930).

LOWER FEDERAL COURT

Hammond v. *Hull,* 76 App. D. C. 301, 131 F. 2d 23 (1942).

Keefe v. *Dulles*, 222 Fed. Reporter, 2d, 390 (1954) Writ of Certiorari denied, Feb. 28, 1955, 75 S. Ct. 440.
Overholser v. *De Marcos*, 149 F. 2d 23 (1945) CC. A. D. C. Writ of Certiorari denied 323 U.S. 889; rehearing denied 326 U.S. 805.
Houghton v. *Ickes*, 101 F. 2d 248 (1938).
United States v. *Bayard*, 16 D. C. 428 (1887), 5 Machey's Rpts 428.
Yee Giving Mee v. *Acherm*, D. C. N. D. Cal. S.D. 108 F. Supp. 502 (1952).

INTERNATIONAL CLAIMS

U.S.A. (John D. Chase) v. United Mexican States, Opinions of Comm'rs (1929) 17.
U.S.A. v. Mexico (Chattin), Opinions of Comm'rs (1927) 422.
U.S.A. (W. H. Falkner) v. United Mexican States, Opinions of Comm'rs (1927) 86.
U.S.A. (L. F. Neer) v. United Mexican States, Opinions of Comm'rs (1926), 71.
U.S.A. v. Mexico (Parrish), Opinions of Comm'rs (1927) 473.
U.S.A. (Harry Roberts) v. United Mexican States, Opinions of Comm'rs (1927) 100.

OTHER

Acts of The Conference For The Codification of International Law, held at The Hague from March 13th to April 12th 1930, Vol. IV, Minutes of the Third Committee, *Responsibility of States For Damages Caused in Their Territory to the Person or Property of Foreigners*, League of Nations Document No. C 351(C). M. 145 (C), 1930. V.
International Conferences of American States 1889–1928.
International Conferences of American States 1933–1940.
International Conference of American States, First Supplement 1933–1940.
Hearings Before the Committee on Foreign Relations, United States Senate, 83rd Cong., 1st Sess., On Status of Forces of the North Atlantic Treaty (June 24, 1953).
Hearings Before a Sub-Committee of the Committee on Armed Services on the Operation of Article VII, NATO Status of Forces Treaty, United States Senate, 35th Cong., 2d Sess., July 29, 1958.
Hearings on the Operation of Article VII, NATO Status of Forces Treaty, 86th Cong., 2d sess., June 8, 1960.
Senate Report No. 1041, 87th Cong., 1st sess., Sept. 15, 1961, on the Operation of Article VII, NATO Status of Forces Treaty.
Proceedings Second Summer Conference on International Law, Cornell Law School, Ithaca, New York, June 23–25, 1958.

INDEX

GPSR Compliance

The European Union's (EU) General Product Safety Regulation (GPSR) is a set of rules that requires consumer products to be safe and our obligations to ensure this.

If you have any concerns about our products, you can contact us on ProductSafety@springernature.com

In case Publisher is established outside the EU, the EU authorized representative is:

Springer Nature Customer Service Center GmbH
Europaplatz 3
69115 Heidelberg, Germany

Batch number: 10830943

Printed by Printforce, the Netherlands